Lord, find me a parking place!

Also by Derek Wood
and published by IVP

The Barnabas Factor
The Jacob Portfolio
The Adam and Eve Agenda

Lord, find me a parking place!

Derek Wood

Inter-Varsity Press

INTER-VARSITY PRESS
38 De Montfort Street, Leicester LE1 7GP, England

First published 1995

British Library Cataloguing in Publication Data
A catalogue record for this book is available from the British Library.

ISBN 0-85110-880-6

Set in Linotron Baskerville
Photoset in Great Britain by
Parker Typesetting Service, Leicester
Printed and bound in Great Britain by
Cox & Wyman Ltd, Reading, Berkshire

Inter-Varsity Press is the book-publishing division of the Universities and Colleges Christian Fellowship (formerly the Inter-Varsity Fellowship), a student movement linking Christian Unions in universities and colleges throughout the United Kingdom and the Republic of Ireland, and a member movement of the International Fellowship of Evangelical Students. For information about local and national activities write to UCCF, 38 De Montfort Street, Leicester LE1 7GP.

Contents

*For Derrick who has helped me
to think through many of the
issues raised in this book.*

CHAPTER 1

Furry green creatures on springs

———————————

Aunt Freda has recently passed her driving test. Aunt Freda is a delightful, rather dotty, middle-aged lady, just under five feet tall. Passers-by have been startled to see her approaching because at first sight the car appears to have no driver. But there she is, clutching the steering wheel and peering over the top of it. To travel as a passenger with Aunt Freda is an alarming experience.

On the windscreen, just above the speedometer, there sits a creature of no species known to zoology. It is furry and a hideous green with spikes of orange hair and is mounted on a spring so that it bobs about in an infuriating way whenever the car is in motion. She calls it George. For most people George would be an annoying distraction to a driver – he certainly annoys the passengers – but Aunt Freda would never be without him. Plunging heedlessly into city-centre traffic she has so far found that all the other drivers keep out of her way. This phenomenon she attributes to George.

Most of us avoid the city centre of course, but Aunt Freda has always shopped at Bigbody's, ever since it was a corner shop. Now it is a huge department store on an island site, surrounded by double yellow lines, 'no parking' signs and meters. But Aunt Freda is not dismayed. She points her car at the maelstrom of traffic and says, 'Now come on, George. Parking place, please!' It seldom fails. Time after time a car will draw out of one of the few available spaces just as she approaches. George is a winner every time.

'Lord, find me a parking place!'

The irony of all this is that Uncle James, Freda's husband, is a vicar. And he is not only disgusted at what he calls his wife's gross superstition but he rarely misses an opportunity to tell her so.

Now it so happened on a wet winter's afternoon that James accepted a lift into town with one of his parishioners, a woman of renown in the church, much respected for her faith. The traffic was worse even than usual, and after three circuits round the one-way system James heard his driver muttering, 'Lord, find me a parking place!' Almost at once he spotted a car-space between two delivery vans.

'Whoopee! Praise the Lord!' They made a bee-line for the space . . . and collided. Violently. With Freda.

So, if it is so wrong and superstitious to expect a furry animal on a spring to find you a parking place, why should it be right to pray to God for the same thing?

Well, for a start, the furry animal has no power to find you a space. If it seems to work, it's all in your imagination. But wait a minute. Has anyone run a test to see whether this is true? To arrive at a satisfactory result it would be necessary for hundreds of superstitious people with Georges in their cars to be timed as to how long it took them to find a parking space, appealing only to their furry animals. Then hundreds of Christians, relying on prayer, would have to be tested in the same way. The results would probably show no significant difference.

In that case we should ask, what's the point of praying to God for a parking place if you might as well pray to a furry animal and get the same result? Or perhaps people who don't pray at all will be more successful than either!

If the Christians *did* show a distinct improvement on the others, we should have to ask why they are being so selfish as to use the unfair advantage they have in condemning their neighbours, whom they should be loving, to be searching the streets in vain.

We need to get back to basics here. What makes it right for us to pray for *anything*? And what expectation should we have that we shall receive it? At one extreme, if we take the 'Find me a parking place' argument to its logical conclusion, all prayer of this kind would appear to be pure idolatry, attempting to use God to obtain what we want; a kind of high-powered superstition. It's natural to most people perhaps to pray when in need, but on this argument alone surely it must be selfish and wrong-headed.

At the other extreme, though, we must hear the words of Jesus of Nazareth,

> 'I will do whatever you ask in my name, so that the Father may be glorified in the Son. If in my name you ask me for anything, I will do it' (John 14:13–14).

There are no ifs and buts there: 'whatever . . . anything . . . I will do it'. Christians cannot ignore such clear and direct words from their Saviour and Lord. So how does that apply to asking for a parking place?

Prayer is for the helpless

We may well find a clue in that classic book, *Prayer*, by O. Hallesby (IVP, 1948). He asks what is that attitude of heart which God recognizes as prayer. Without hesitation he puts helplessness at the top of the list. He writes on page 13:

This is unquestionably the first and the surest indication of a praying heart. As far as I can see, prayer has been ordained only for the helpless. It is the last resort of the helpless; indeed, the very last way out. We try everything before we finally resort to prayer.

This is not only true of us before our conversion. Prayer is our last resort also throughout our whole Christian life. I know very well that we offer many and beautiful prayers, both privately and publicly, without helplessness as the impelling power. But I am not at all positive that this is prayer. Prayer and helplessness are inseparable. Only he who is helpless can truly pray.

So we now have three pertinent questions to ask when we are minded to pray for something:

1. Is it superstitious? Am I tempted to pray because I fear that things will go wrong if I don't? Am I using God as an idol to get what I want?

2. Is it 'in the name of Christ'? This was the limitation that Jesus gave: 'I will do whatever you ask . . . If in *my name* you ask . . .' What does this mean? His answer was, 'so that the Father may be glorified in the Son'. So will my prayer, if answered, bring glory to the Father?

3. Am I truly helpless, or is this a routine matter, because I think I ought to bring God into it (it's the Christian thing), but which I could manage quite well without him really?

Now all this puts a different complexion on things. Perhaps it's not a black-and-white question, 'Ought I to pray for a parking place?' Perhaps the answer depends on your attitude and the specific circumstances.

On the one hand take Charles, the up-and-coming young executive who has a meeting at the town hall at 11.00 am. His office is some way across town so he takes his car. He usually expects to be frantically busy, though this morning he finds he has got up to date by 10.30. Instead of leaving at once he pauses for a cup of coffee and leaves at 10.45. There is a car park ten minutes' walk away from the town hall and Charles can claim for such expenses, but it's too late now and he arrives in Town Hall Square at 10.57. No problem. Charles is a Christian. 'All things work together for good for those who love God' (Romans 8:28).

Whether Charles gets away with this one is not the point. But how does he measure up to the three questions? It looks very much as if he is using God as a means to get something which he could have provided for himself. Is he bringing glory to God the Father? Perhaps he wants to 'witness' to his business associates. 'Do you know God found me a parking place this morning? I was late getting here' (why?) 'and I'm sure the car-park was full,' (it wasn't actually, but he hadn't been to look) 'so I just prayed and there it was' (he hadn't noticed in his hurry that the words 'RE-SERVED: MAYOR ONLY' were written in large white letters on the road). And was he truly helpless? By 10:57 he probably was, but it was his fault that it happened that way.

On the other hand take Jane. She is desperately finding her way through the traffic to the furniture shop. She is taking her elderly mother to choose a new armchair (probably her last as she has a severe heart condition). The furniture shop is in a busy street with cars parked on both sides and mother can walk only a few yards. Jane prays for a space. Whether she finds one is not the question here but whether she is right to ask. She has done everything she could, but in the end she needs help. She is helpless.

So there are no rules restricting what we should or should not pray for. If God is indeed our Father he surely wants us to share all our joys and fears with him, but our attitude and the particular circumstances make a great deal of difference. We shall return to this question in chapter six.

Providence

Praying about parking spaces can be the subject of flippant remarks or it can be a serious business, but it is not usually a question of life and death. Safety in travel is just that. How often and earnestly we pray for the safety of ourselves and our friends or relations as we thunder through the air, float over the depths of the sea or jockey our way through swiftly moving traffic. Surely it is right, and God expects it of us, to commit our loved ones into his care and protection. It is natural for us to pray for safety and there are wonderful stories of people who have been saved from horrendous accidents. Some have been delayed and missed the aircraft that crashed; others have emerged unscathed from the burning motorbus.

But not always. Some years ago in Thailand a minibus, carrying missionaries and their families, was involved in a road accident and five dedicated Christians were killed (and seven children), people who were instrumental to the running of the hospital at Manorom. Why? Had not prayer been offered for their safety? Perhaps. But are we to believe in a God who removes his protection from his servants, in proportion to the lack of prayer from their friends? And how much prayer is needed to keep a minibus on the road? This question is ridiculous. No. God does not guarantee to keep his servants free from accidents. When they happen the best we can do is to ask, 'What can we learn from this dreadful tragedy?'

But, before we write off the need for prayer for protection, let us remember those occasions when the good hand of God *has* saved his people (and perhaps others who have not bothered to pray: the Lord sends good and bad weather equally to the just and the unjust). Consider also how many times we must have been saved from accidents without knowing it. How often have we stepped into the road and been narrowly missed by a passing vehicle? How often have we found our attention wandering or our eyes closing while driving and been grateful that no obstacles were about? In fact, we might look at it from the other end of the telescope and express gratitude for every passing day that we escape *without* a serious accident. That would be more positive than blaming God for neglecting us when we do suffer from one.

Our questioning whether our prayers are in danger of being based on superstition has led us face to face with what Christians have called Providence. Back in Reformation times the rulers of Heidelberg set down a definition of providence in the 'Heidelberg Catechism' of 1563:

> Question 27. *What do you understand by the providence of God?*
> The almighty and ever-present power of God whereby he still upholds, as it were by his own hand, heaven and earth together with all creatures, and rules in such a way that leaves and grass, rain and drought, fruitful and unfruitful years, food and drink, health and sickness, riches and poverty, and everything else, come to us not by chance but by his fatherly hand.
> Question 28. *What advantage comes from acknowledging God's creation providence?*
> We learn that we are to be patient in adversity, grateful in the midst of blessing, and to trust our faithful God and Father for the future, assured

that no creature shall separate us from his love, since all creatures are so completely in his hand that without his will they cannot even move.

(Quoted in Mark Noll [ed.] *Confessions and Catechisms of the Reformation*, IVP, 1992)

These answers are very carefully worded. The providence of God does not offer us instant answers to all our personal wants, in fact we may find ourselves 'in adversity' and need patience (not escape). Providence does not, on the other hand, teach that everything that happens is the will of God, a kind of fatalism which says 'whatever will be will be' and there's nothing that we (or God?) can do about it.

No, providence, by this definition, is supremely a question of *relationship*. God, as creator, continues to interact with his handiwork: plant, animal and human. His will is constantly interweaving with what is going on. Our response must be neither to ignore him nor to try to use him, but to depend on him as a child on a father, believing neither in his malevolence nor his indifference but in his love for us.

The world is so constructed and has so developed that we cannot dispassionately prove the providence of God, but neither can it be denied. It is there for the faithful to discern; a loving, giving-and-taking relationship with God.

Conclusion

So what shall we say about praying for a parking place? Rabbi Blue, gentle philosopher and broadcaster, has a favourite saying, 'Don't take it too heavy, dear.' There's no need to get worked up about whether we do or do not pray for such things. God loves us to be in close touch with him, and what worries us worries him too. So, go on, pray.

The question is not what do we pray for, parking places, good weather for the garden party, safety in travel or little Harry's measles, but *how* we pray. Are we humbly dependent on God our Father whom we love, or are we arrogantly presuming upon that love to serve us?

No prayer will ever be totally pure and unmixed with selfishness this side of heaven, so the debate cannot be simplified into blacks and whites. But that is no excuse for us to relax and carry on doing our own thing as if it didn't matter.

We must examine some other areas of life where this self-centred, manipulating attitude has infiltrated, and we need to try to answer the question: Why am I so prone to want everything to work out well for *me*? We shall return to this question in chapter three. But first we must be clearer about what we mean by using God as an idol.

CHAPTER 2

The idol factory

I had a dream. In my dream I met an angel and he invited me to visit an idol factory (odd things happen in dreams). I realized that I'd never seen an idol factory before, so I agreed to go. As we drew near it became obvious that the building we were approaching had been designed as a church.

'What a tragedy', I said, 'that a church should have been abandoned like this and used as an idol factory.'

'The tragedy is worse than you think,' said the angel.

We went inside and I was astonished to find no evidence of idol manufacture at all. There were just rows of pews, a pulpit, a reading desk and a communion table and no signs of the making of anything. I turned to my guide. 'But this is a church,' I said, 'you said it was an idol factory. Or do you mean to suggest that the statue of Jesus or the picture of Mary and the Christ-child are idols and are worshipped?'

'No,' said my guide, 'there is no danger that the people who use this building will worship the statue or the picture. But you are quite right. This *is* a church. And it always has been. But it is also an idol factory.'

I assumed that he meant that the factory was hidden away in the crypt or even the roof (one can be quite intelligent in dreams sometimes), but that was not what the angel had in mind.

'The tragedy is', he went on, 'that the people who use this church worship God. You think that is no tragedy?

It ought not to be. But they idolize him. By that I don't mean that they adore him; that would be quite in order. No. They use him as an idol. An idol is the invention of a human being, something made by a man or woman, and invested with imaginary powers. So the idol-worshippers pray to their idol, bring offerings and behave so that they will please the idol. Then they expect an appropriate response – good luck, success at the office, plenty to eat and drink, a happy marriage.'

'I realize this,' I said impatiently, 'but you said that these people worshipped God. He is not an idol.'

'Quite so,' said the angel, 'the real God, creator of the universe, is not an idol. But you still haven't grasped the point. The god these people worship is the construct of their own imaginations. They have made a god in their own image and they give that image great powers. They pray to him and bring offerings that they hope will please him. And they behave well and they hope he will be friendly towards them. Then they expect to get their fair reward. Having won his approval they think he will look after them in every way that they think proper. And the worst of it is,' he said, holding up his hand to prevent my interrupting him, 'they sincerely believe that it is the real God they are treating like this. Did I not tell you it was a tragic situation?'

'But,' I heard myself saying, 'but, but . . .' and I found that I couldn't speak. And suddenly the important thing I was going to say didn't make any sense. And I awoke. And, as the King James Version would have put it so delightfully, 'Behold, it was a dream'. A very disturbing dream though and one not to be forgotten easily.

Even allowing for the fact that the dream (or night-mare) church was an extreme case, is there not some-thing of the idol factory in all our worship, our prayer, our relationship with God, our need for guidance, for peace of mind, everything we do? This must make us pause and ask a basic question: How Christian am I? Is my faith only a veneer which covers the real pagan idolater underneath?

Isaiah and the timber-shop

Straightforward idolatry, making a statue and worshipping it, is not a problem for most Western Christians. There is more of it in Asia than in Europe. Idolatry was condemned by the commandment in Exodus 20:4–6 in no uncertain terms:

> You shall not make for yourself an idol, whether in the form of anything that is in heaven above, or that is on the earth beneath, or that is in the water under the earth. You shall not bow down to them or worship them; for I the LORD your God am a jealous God, punishing children for the iniquity of parents, to the third and the fourth generation of those who reject me, but showing steadfast love to the thousandth generation of those who love me and keep my commandments.

Idolatry is the sin of hating God and we usually interpret it as worship of things, or even people, in God's place: cars, houses, pop stars (are they not called 'idols'?), money, status, security and so forth. But although these things do tend to take the place of God and are expected to provide satisfaction, they are not really idols in the sense that we have carved them and bring offerings to them and expect them to help us. Certainly they are not the chief issues which will concern us in this book.

The classic form of idolatry was denounced by the Old Testament prophets in terms of ridicule. Listen to Isaiah in chapter 44. Here is a part of it:

> [The carpenter] ... makes a god and worships it,
> makes it a carved image and bows down before it.
> Half of [the wood] he burns in the fire; over this
> half he roasts meat, eats it and is satisfied. He also
> warms himself and says, 'Ah, I am warm; I can feel
> the fire!' The rest of it he makes into a god, his idol,
> bows down to it and worships it; he prays to it and
> says, 'Save me, for you are my god!' (Isaiah 44:15–
> 17).

Generations of Bible readers have read these words
and others like them with great merriment. It is a
devastating exposure of the folly of making and
worshipping idols, and those who feel safe from such
errors are inclined to indulge in some relatively innocent amusement at the expense of the benighted pag-
ans. Certainly it is a shocking thing to use a block of
wood as a god.

But even that is better than using God as a block of
wood!

Using God, that is the essence of the problem. How
can we, who were created by God, dare to use him as a
means to getting things done as we want? And, if this is
really the danger that we face, how did we get here, so
that we can find a way back out again?

The waxen god of the mountains

The story is told of a very remote village high on a
mountain pass. High as it was the village was over-
shadowed by towering peaks and at the summit of the
tallest was a shrine. In the shrine sat a god made of
wax, wonderfully crafted long ages ago, and this god
was worshipped by the villagers. Sited as it was, thousands of feet above the village, the shrine was well-nigh
inaccessible. In fact only at midsummer, when the
snows had melted, could it be reached. Then the

Chosen, the team of young and strong villagers who could endure the climb, made the annual pilgrimage to the summit, bringing offerings and the prayers of the people. Many people in that place lived their whole life without seeing their god. It was sufficient that news of it was brought back by the pilgrims.

It so happened that a young man, who had been away from the village and received some education, was passed over and not chosen as a pilgrim. In his disappointment he began to think and to reason. If he could not go up to the god why could the god not be brought down to him? In fact, consider the advantage of such a move. It would be very difficult to execute such a manoeuvre it was true, but once the god was down in the village there would no longer be a need to choose pilgrims, which had always led to the great disappointment of those not chosen. There would be no need for the long and dangerous climb to the pinnacle where the shrine was perched (more than once in recent years there had been fatal accidents). And, most important of all, the god would be accessible to everyone. It could be placed at the centre of the village where it belonged and everyone, old and young alike, could bring their offerings and prayers every day if they wished. It was well known that blessings depend on the amount of offerings made. The offerings, and the blessings, would be enormous.

As might be expected such a revolutionary (some said 'blasphemous') idea was not easily accepted. Those who opposed it on religious grounds found it very difficult to deny the obvious good sense of the proposal, so they took refuge in pointing out that the removal of the shrine would be impossible.

The young progressives who had now emerged were already planning devices of ropes and pulleys, trestles and beams, and were confident that they could achieve their aim. After all, they said, the shrine was carried up there however many years ago, so it was not beyond the wit of modern people to carry it down again. The sheer rationalism of this argument shocked many of the older folk who believed that the shrine had always been on the mountain top, as long as the mountain had existed and certainly ages before the village appeared.

The debate split the village into two factions, the Old Believers and the New Believers, and gradually the New Believers gathered strength and power until the Head Man was converted to their ideas. That year, when midsummer came round, the pilgrimage became a working party. It would be tedious to describe how that expedition succeeded in bringing the shrine with its holy burden down the mountain, cliff, cleft and scree, stair and track, but finally the god was placed at the centre of the village square, on a plinth specially prepared for it. The whole population went wild with a mixture of dreadful fear lest their daring should be rewarded with disaster, and hilarious joy that their god was now amongst them (and, it must be added, for some at least a degree of smug satisfaction at their own cleverness).

For some time all went remarkably well. As expected offerings were generous and the village in return prospered. No-one was struck down for their impertinence, in fact the god began to be regarded with affection rather than awe. It was a part of the landscape of the village and everyone nodded to it as they passed by on their daily business.

This happy state of affairs continued for some years, though the careful observer would have noticed that the offerings became scarcer and the worshippers less devout and it became customary not to nod as one passed the shrine. It seemed rather superstitious.

Then one very hot summer a change began to take

place. The god was seen to lean a little and appeared to be shrinking. Someone, greatly daring, leaned over and touched the hem of his waxen robe. It was soft. The god was melting! There was nothing they could do about it. The weather remained unbearably hot for weeks on end and water was as scarce as gold leaf. There could be no question of cooling their god with water, as some suggested.

Soon there was nothing but a mound of dark purple wax slowly spilling over the edge of the plinth. No-one could worship a heap of warm wax. As the days grew shorter and the weather became cooler, bolder spirits came to the edge of the mound and took wax for their oil lamps to light their homes. Before the end of that winter there was no god, only a plinth. Some years later the plinth was removed to make way for a railway track.

The radical shift

An everyday story of the errors of pagan belief you may say; but this story can be interpreted in different ways. There are three phases in the development (or degeneration) of the villagers' worship. In the first stage, there was awe and reverence. A pilgrimage to the shrine was an event of great significance; to be chosen as a pilgrim was the privilege of a lifetime.

The second stage saw the radical shift from their serving the god to making the god serve them. The tables were completely turned. Without realizing what they were doing, in fact with very laudable motives, they reversed the true order of things, 'tamed' their god and set it to work for them. They literally brought it down to their level.

The third and final stage came as an inevitable result of the second. Their reverence became respect, which turned to carelessness and finally they ignored the shrine altogether. As soon as they tried to use the idol and control it they destroyed it. The mystery had gone. It was there only for a limited purpose and if it failed in its purpose they had no further use for it. They ignored its true nature and allowed it to fade away.

So where do these pictures of idolatry lead us? What has all this to do with Christian worship at the end of the twentieth century? If we take the three scenes in reverse order we may say that if a religion has degenerated to the stage of the religious using their god as an idol then the religion is in a steep decline and may not have long to live. Isaiah's vivid description of the folly of idol worship uncovers the hollow unreality of such a practice. And my dream sounded a warning that perhaps the Christian church is in danger of sliding into this danger of trying to make use of God as an idol, making him in our own image.

If this diagnosis is true then Western Christianity is more or less on its way out, and rapidly shrinking religious observance would bear out this terrifying scenario. In Britain, for example, church membership has been declining steadily at around 4% every five years (see detailed figures in *UK Christian Handbook* [MARC Europe, 1992–93 edition]). The figures represent purely numbers and leave untouched the authenticity or otherwise of the members' beliefs. Even so, the picture looks dark.

However, the real God is not made of wax and will not melt, and it is the faith of the church that he will not abandon his people. But it should be helpful to examine some of the evidences of our decline into idolatry so that we can be aware of it, avoid its entanglements and co-operate with our God in reversing the trend. And that is what this book is about.

CHAPTER 3

'Me first!'

'Now I belong to Jesus, Jesus belongs to me.'
(Norman J. Clayton)

'I am his and he is mine for ever and for ever.'
(James Grindlay Small)

Hymns and songs have celebrated the close relationship between the Lord and his people as individuals very much as if it were a marriage relationship: 'we belong to one another'. The Bible frequently describes God and his people as married to one another, though the 'bride' (*e.g.* Revelation 21:2) is the people of God in the plural, the church, not the individual. So it may be stretching it a bit to talk about Jesus *belonging* to me. If the balancing 'I belong to Jesus' is kept firmly on the agenda perhaps no harm can come of it.

When the 'he belongs to me' element is emphasized at the expense of the other, however, we are already sliding towards the 'George factor', seeing God as our own possession and useful to us in ways that we choose. How did we get into this situation? Has it always existed or is it of recent origin? If we could understand where it comes from we would be better able to overcome it.

The fish's-eye view

This is where we need to exercise some imagination, which is no easy option. Can you think what it is like to be a fish? Living, of course, in water. The fish doesn't know that it lives in water because it has never experienced anything else. So if you were able to tell it that its environment is water it might not believe you. At best it would say, 'Yes, of course. So what?' Water is so natural to the fish that (even if it had an imagination) it could imagine nothing else.

We are totally surrounded by a philosophy of life which takes it for granted that 'I' am an individual first and foremost (an integral part of a family perhaps, but basically me). Everything revolves round me. I am the most important aspect of this world to me, as you are to you. It is assumed by most people, especially in the media world, whence we imbibe the majority of our assumptions, that I have a right to be happy, to be successful, to be healthy and to be fulfilled. If I choose to believe in a god, that's OK but that's my private affair, my hobby, if you like. And the means I use to achieve success, health, happiness and fulfilment are my affair too, so no sermons please.

Now take a deep breath and try to imagine a society where things were very different. Where the most important element was God. Where I have a place in the hierarchy of things and a *duty* to live in accordance with God's providence. This life is but a vale of tears which leads into the glory hereafter (if we survive the Judgment) and I do not expect health or happiness, except as a bonus, for which I am deeply grateful.

We are back in medieval Europe. No, I am not calling for the clocks to be put back. In many ways they were terrible times: brutal wars and crusades, devastating epidemics, pain, dirt and disease and widespread illiteracy, superstition and fear . . . Neither were morals necessarily different from those of today, especially if the private and often public lives of monarchs, popes, cardinals and bishops is anything to go by.

My point though is this. God was generally acknowledged to be supreme. Most people knew their secure place in society. Duties and responsibilities were clearly defined. People often fell short of the high standards which the church taught them, but they knew they were falling short, and they confessed it and some were even ashamed about it. Many of the rich tried to bribe God to accept them into heaven by their endowments of monasteries or payments for masses to be said for their souls, but many too were the prayers selflessly prayed for the souls (and bodies) of other people. They tried perhaps to propitiate God, but dared not try to use him. He was too real and too big for that.

The radical change that has occurred in Western society in the last five or six hundred years began imperceptibly slowly, gathered momentum in the eighteenth and nineteenth centuries, and has found full expression by the end of the twentieth. To examine how it has happened would require a history book, but let's look at a few of the milestones.

Telling it like it is

1513. Enter Nicolo Machiavelli with his book, *Principe*. The Prince. This was an account of how the modern statesman should achieve and hold on to political and economic power. The important point was not how he did it but that he did it. Machiavelli was not opposed to private virtue; he praised it, but it must not interfere with politics. Paying lip service to divine institutions like the papacy and the Holy Roman Empire might be helpful to assist one's rise in the world, but these were not basic. Neither was God. Machiavelli was perhaps the first to be open and, some would say, honest enough to see things not as they ought to be but as they actually were. People are corrupt and corrupt means are needed to rule them.

All this gave us the word 'Machiavellian' of course, the doctrine that the end justifies the means. What is alarming is that so much of it reads like old hat today. At the time it caused a tremendous outcry. It was blasphemous, brutal, cynical and abhorrent.

We move on a century or so.

In 1650, during the English Civil War, Englishman Thomas Hobbes produced his *Leviathan*. Those were the days when it was popular to speculate on the nature of the state and its government and how it came about. It was assumed that there was once upon a time a 'state of nature' out of which politics grew. The most celebrated 'state of nature' was to be Frenchman Rousseau's in the next century, where the Noble Savage lived in idyllic bliss, only to be spoilt by civilization. But Hobbes's state of nature was by no means idyllic. Like Machiavelli he drew the picture not as it ought to be but as he thought it was. Human nature was twisted and evil. The life of man had been 'solitary, poor, nasty, brutish and short'. So it was a matter of self-interest for people to band together to defend themselves against each other and try to make it social, rich, pleasant, humane and long.

That may sound sensible to our ears that have been used to rational arguments and humanist assumptions, but again, it caused a major disturbance in mid-seventeenth-century England and Hobbes had to withdraw from public life for eleven years. Yes, he was a tall and genial man, whose chief exercise was found in playing tennis which he did until he was over seventy years of age, but he was regarded by the church and by many of his compatriots as an infidel and very dangerous. It is perhaps significant that he found some to support him and agree with his ideas about human nature and the need for force to curb it. Realism was gaining round and idealism was losing it.

The right to happiness

A century and a quarter after *Leviathan* comes another important work, on economics this time, by a Scotsman, Adam Smith, entitled, *An Inquiry into the Nature and Causes of the Wealth of Nations*. He believed, one might almost say passionately, in free trade. In the eighteenth century, nations tended to safeguard their own trade by imposing tariffs, taxes on imports, in the belief that they could win a bigger share in a market which was limited, a larger slice in the world's cake. Smith claimed that the cake was infinitely expandable if only nations would abandon protectionism and allow trade to circulate freely.

He believed too in the division of labour, so that those who were good at something supplied the world with it and, with the proceeds, bought what they needed from other experts (an excellent plan unless you have a world war). The basis of his scheme was human acquisitiveness (some would say 'greed') and ambition. Allow all this energy to have free rein, he said, and wealth will flourish. The poor will be driven by their poverty to make greater efforts and will be rewarded. By the rich? Yes, but only because it is in their *interest* to have a fit and able work-force. It was all overseen by the Unseen Hand of Providence.

Smith was making a virtue of human selfishness and ambition and elevating it into a system of economics, which has its supporters to this day. One may be for-given, two and a quarter centuries on, for asking what happened to the Unseen Hand of Providence which was supposed to look after the poor, but his ideas have formed the basis of much modern economic theory. And he was not accused of blasphemy or insulting humanity. The reasonable, open-minded society of eighteenth-century England lionized him.

In the same year that the *Wealth of Nations* was published, 1776, Thomas Jefferson's draft for the Declaration of Independence was polished and accepted as the foundation for the United States, on July 4th of that year. It opened with these stirring words:

> We hold these truths to be self-evident – 'That all men are created equal; that they are endowed by their Creator with certain unalienable rights; that among these are life, liberty and the pursuit of happiness ... Whenever any form of government becomes destructive of these ends, it is the right of the people to alter or to abolish it, and to institute new government, laying its foundations on such principles ... as to them seem most likely to effect their safety and happiness.'

Note three phrases, 'self-evident', 'unalienable rights' and 'safety and happiness.' They sound eminently reasonable, and that is just what they are, but it would be interesting to know by what authority the Congress decided what the Creator has given us. Is self-evidence enough? Does the Bible state anywhere that we have 'unalienable rights'? Is government to be left to the whim of the people and what to them seems 'most likely to effect their safety and happiness'? Modern democracy is built on these foundations: what was 'self-evident', a demand for rights and the pursuit of happiness.

But Europe has kept its ancient traditions. Has it? Within thirteen years the French Revolution had overthrown the monarchy and published, in August 1789, the 'Declaration of the Rights of Man', much derived from the American example, and revolutions and evolution during the last century and this have resulted in many old foundations being dug up. Where the old forms remain, new demands for self-determination, rights of all kinds and the quest for happiness have grown up round them and engulfed them.

Is anything wrong with happiness then? Of course not. God wants us to be happy, 'blessed', fortunate, fulfilled (there's a whole chapter on this later), but true happiness is the result of pursuing some higher purpose. The pursuit of happiness for its own sake is doomed to failure. Yet, this too was elevated into a philosophy in the nineteenth century and given an academic sounding name, 'Utilitarianism'.

It was Jeremy Bentham, a lawyer, who in 1817 published his *Catechism of Parliamentary Reform*. His sharp, precise mind asked a basic question of every law or institution, 'What is the use of it?' And how did he decide what was and was not useful? The useful was that which helped to produce the 'greatest happiness of the greatest number'.

It seems a small step now to modern twentieth-century democracy, based on the (assumed) will of the people, which is to increase happiness by means of economic progress, in which the end may well justify the means, in which we must use force to protect ourselves against each other, where rights are everything and duty is a concept to be laughed at, where self-expression, consumerism, self-fulfilment and above all the total absence of God seem to be quite normal.

Late in 1993 British Prime Minister John Major announced a policy of 'Back to Basics'. The grand old virtues were to be emphasized once more. Britain would become 'great' again, a place we could be proud to live in. It sounded hopeful.

Of course in a multi-faith society we could hardly expect the virtues and values to be specifically Christian. But then all good Moslems, Hindus, Jews, Sikhs and even those of no religion value honesty, faithfulness, justice, family unity and so on. But a flurry of scandals involving senior members of John Major's party drew down further disclaimers. Oh no, 'Back to Basics' was not about *morals*, certainly not personal morals. No witch-hunts. No trials by tabloid. Anyway 'morality' is not a politically correct idea nowadays. No, that is not the kind of value we are talking about. So what is? Opposition leader John Smith raised that very question in the House of Commons on 11th January 1994. Mr Major was in Brussels at the time. The Leader of the House, Mr Tony Newton, rose to reply. Now we should know.

'Our concern', said Mr Newton, 'is with raising standards in education, strengthening the fight against crime and *above all* [my italics] with strengthening the British economy.'

So the bottom line, the real substance of the grand old values that we all long to return to, is strengthening the British economy. And to do that we must improve education and combat crime. 'It was a dire afternoon for the Government,' wrote Robert Hardman in the *Daily Telegraph* the following day. 'Mr Major was probably glad to be in Belgium.'

Western civilization is suffering a long dire afternoon, and travelling to Belgium, or to the moon for that matter, will not save us from its consequences. Religion is out. Morality is out. There remain these three: education, the fight against crime and the British economy. But the greatest of these is the British economy . . .

Babel rebuilt

The story is told of a devastated world, after the Third World War, and the only inhabitants remaining are two chimpanzees. One offers the other an apple. The other says, 'Oh no! Don't start all that again!'

We are not starting quite as far back as primeval chaos, but we are back into the world of Genesis 11 and the Tower of Babel. The godless men of that time were ill-content and wanted to make a name for themselves, to do something that would leave its mark on the world. So they got together and pooled all their technological resources and built a tower that would reach to heaven. And God came down to look at it (he had to come 'down' because, although they hoped to reach up to heaven, he couldn't even see it from where he was) and God said, 'This will not do. There is no end to what they might do.' And he confused their language and scattered them (Genesis 11:1–9).

Those people were not terribly wicked, neither were the writers and thinkers we have been looking at. They all acted from the best of motives with the good of their fellow humans at heart. But, like the men of the Plain at Shinar, they left God out and invented new reasons for our existence, other than the praise and love and glory of God. David Atkinson in his comment on the Babel story in *The Message of Genesis 1–11* (IVP, 1990, p. 182), says, 'If you will live without God at the centre, you will have no centre at all.'

This is a profound statement. It is not that modern civilization has removed God from the centre and put something else in his place, nor even that the centre is now empty and awaiting a tenant. *There is no centre left.* It has gone. God has been replaced, not by a single idol but by many, pluralist, relativist idols. Nothing ultimately matters any more. There is no such thing as Truth, and we are lost . . .

Swimming in modernism

Now whatever has all this to do with asking God for a parking place or for safety on our train journey? Much in every way. It is clear that the principles (if that's the right word), the basic assumptions of modern society, are totally at odds with the Christian faith as set out in the New Testament: God at the centre; Christ the supreme example of self-sacrifice and our sin-bearer; the purpose of life to love, serve and forgive; to give and not to grasp; to see this life as a pilgrim-way leading to a better life after death ... All of this is meaningless to the modern (or some would like to use the jargon word 'post-modern') man or woman.

So we would expect the churches to be shining beacons of truth in the midst of all this darkness, set apart by the completeness of the opposites, as far from the world as east is from west, as different as glowing warmth from gnawing cold. But it is not so. These 'modern' ideas have seeped into our churches, have leaked in, gradually filling them so that we, like the fish with which we began this chapter, are swimming in an enclosed world of 'modern' thinking. We use Christian terminology but act in modern ways. We pray to the God of the cross to come in power to help us. We ask the Saviour who had nowhere to lay his head to provide us with comfortable homes. Our church services are often conducted as though we had no duty to worship but only a right to be happy. In short, we use God as yet another convenient invention of the consumer society.

Many Christians are becoming increasingly aware of this appalling situation and are turning back to some of the old wisdom of silence, contemplation and the pursuit of peace. After engaging with all this confusion and these battles for understanding perhaps it's time that we pause and open ourselves to *shalom*, peace, and get away from the world for a while.

CHAPTER 4

'Stand back'

Tucked away in the first chapter of the prophecy of Joel are the plaintive words, 'surely, joy withers away among the people' (Joel 1:12). The prophet is describing the disastrous effects of a plague of locusts. It is as if the spirit of the people has evaporated. Their purpose and vitality have been sapped.

So it is with many Christians today. The plague of locusts has been a silent, creeping invasion of the world's fashions and thought forms, so that we have lost much of the basic structure of our faith and we approach God not in the glorious freedom of the children of God, but as if he were a cross between a pagan idol and a computerized machine, and surely joy withers away among the people.

Surely we're not going to sit here bewailing our history and bemoaning our fate? Indeed not. Having diagnosed the problem, what are we going to do about it? From now on we shall be more positive, looking for the way back to a wholesome attitude.

'Let's get away'

A feature of the second half of twentieth-century Christendom has been the growth of conferences, retreats and conventions. It is almost a growth industry in some countries. Old mansions are converted into conference centres and retreat houses, hotels are taken over for gatherings of the faithful, holiday camps are booked years ahead to accommodate thousands who flock to 'Gales Week'. In passing, it is interesting that there are enough relatively wealthy Christians to be able to afford these comparative luxuries.

Now the question for us is this: Are these 'Let's get away' activities just one more element in the modern drift, leading us away from true distinctiveness, or are they a wholesome step away from the brink and back to Christian normality?

Uncle James, Freda's husband, has no doubt about it. Freda's sister, Vera, is a rather contemplative soul, quite unlike her sister who takes things as they come and never fails to take them when they do. Vera spends many weekends a year, and much of her pension, in attending retreats. When James is tired of berating his wife about her superstition his wrath will often fall, in her absence anyhow, on Vera. The reader will understand that James is a rather angry man who feels unfulfilled in his calling and who needs the help of a counsellor (which he steadfastly refuses to accept), but that is not central to our tale at the moment.

'It's Vera's birthday on Sunday week,' says Freda. Always willing to be magnanimous James suggests that she should be invited for the day. 'She's going to Bradgate Abbey for the weekend.'

'Not another retreat!'

'Yes.'

'But she went there last week.'

'No, that was Grantley Grange.'

'What's the attraction?'

'Well, she likes the way Magnus Gorringe leads them.'

'That's exactly what I thought. These retreats are nothing but an escapist ego-trip with guru-worship thrown in. They're attended by a gang of geriatrics who can't cope with everyday life. They get to know the favourite leaders on the circuit and flock unquestioningly to hear them. They enjoy the quietness because they're old-fashioned people who couldn't make a noise if they tried and, worst of all, they are led to believe that they're meeting God, when all they're doing is communing with their own inadequacy. It's all a great big con-trick. The best you can say about it is that it's a reasonably harmless way to spend your money.'

'I think that's all rather unkind, James, and young Charlotte goes away to Gales Week every year . . .'

'Oh, that's just the same thing, but it's not silence they're after but noise. Retreats are for aged introverts – Gales Week is for young extroverts. It's all escapism from the real world, getting topped up with the kind of pseudo-spirituality you happen to enjoy. Sitting in silence for an hour is the same as waving your arms about to a rock band. They both pretend to be experiencing God when they're actually deceiving themselves.' And James stumps off to his study to prepare a sermon on knowing God.

Phew!

Is James right in exposing one of Christianity's apparent growth points as really another aspect of idolizing God, using him to get what we want, or is there some positive hope to be found here? Let's look at the motives behind the 'Let's get away' trend and measure them against our idolatry standard.

Escape from the world

It is an enormous relief to arrive at a comfortable conference centre or retreat house, to be welcomed quietly and shown to your room, to know that for a few days at least you will not have to attend to the telephone, the doorbell or the heap of paper that insists on pouring through your letter-box.

It is a great joy to come again to a vast complex of halls, seminar rooms and chalets, to know that everyone here is like-minded, that you can be yourself in choosing your sessions or your free time, worship openly and know that you will not be judged.

Both retreat and convention (shall we call it) create for themselves a world within the world, some would like to say 'a bit of heaven within the world', which emphasizes the sharp contrast between everyday life 'out there' and warm Christian experience 'in here'. The ordinary church-goer, in Western society at least, experiences organized worship for one or more hours a week, perhaps a midweek meeting or two and the fellowship of a few close friends of an evening occasionally. But all this is in the context of the ordinary, everyday secular world at least 90% of the time, where the emphasis is on pressure, acquisitiveness and the pursuit of happiness. And we have already noticed how these pressures have infiltrated the church as well.

So it looks as if we all need to withdraw from the lonely outposts of life on the front line and experience for a while the richer embrace of uninterrupted Christian fellowship for at least a few days. Surely this must be a valid exercise. Ships need to be refitted, cars need to be serviced regularly, houses need to be repainted and surely Christians need to remove themselves from the heat of the secular battle and enjoy some *shalom*, peace, together. This must be so, even if it is seen only as a means of strengthening to endure the further battle ahead.

The Christian need look no further than the example of Jesus Christ, who withdrew, apparently regularly, from 'the world' to be quiet with his Father. He clearly expected his disciples to do the same:

The apostles gathered around Jesus, and told him all that they had done and taught. He said to them, 'Come away to a deserted place all by yourselves and rest awhile.' For many were coming and going, and they had no leisure even to eat. And they went away in the boat to a deserted place by themselves (Mark 6:30–31).

Jesus commands it, reason advises it and our feelings cry out for it; a quiet place for some rest. So surely there's no problem here.

There is one, and that is the danger of coming to rely exclusively on retreats and conventions and to treat the rest of our lives as unfortunate interludes between the high experiences of 'Bradgate Abbey' or 'Gales Week'. It looks as if the rhythm of life that Jesus exemplified was working with the fellowship of the disciples for most of the time, experiencing the presence of God in healing, teaching, compassion and help, worshipping by means of working for the Father in the din and dust of reality; with disciplined withdrawal every now and then for refreshment and re-creation.

The danger signals are the phrases like 'I can really worship God at Grantley Grange' or 'God is *there* at Gales Week but not in my home village' or 'I need to talk to God. I must go to Bradgate Abbey for a week.' The idol is emerging from its cupboard. The idol refuses to be involved in everyday life but must be venerated at the festivals. But God the Holy Spirit is present at all times and does not live in a conference centre or holiday camp. Leaders of retreats and conventions are always warning their customers of this danger, but it remains a danger still. To locate God more intensely in a particular place or in a particular group of people (or in a particularly admired person) is to begin to idolize him.

Listen to God

So there is great value in withdrawing from 'the world' every now and then provided that we keep it in perspective. But what about the positive aspect — what are we withdrawing in order to do? Apart from the peace and quiet aspect (which is as far as some people get) or the achievement of a spiritual zip (which is as far as some others get), the usual answers would be 'to hear God speaking', 'to learn', 'to draw close to God'.

These are admirable purposes and seem more and more necessary as modern life encroaches on our spirituality. We are realizing that the familiar structure of our church services often emphasizes *our* worship, *our* praise, *our* participation, but gives little room for God to speak. Perhaps we hear the Scriptures read (but there's no time to reflect on them) or the Psalms said or sung (but there's no time to experience them) or a sermon preached (but there's no chance to discuss or question what the preacher has decided is God's message for us).

Even in freer gatherings such as prayer meetings, the emphasis has become strongly placed on what we say to God. When does he have a chance to speak to us?

So it is good that the overall picture in Western Christianity is being enriched by the rediscovery of spirituality directed towards what God is saying to us, rather than what we want to say to God. At the risk of oversimplification we could say that Catholic, Charismatic and Evangelical emphases are discernible. God speaks to us through the silence, through the prophet or gifted teacher and through the Scriptures. The enrichment here is that these strands are very rarely seen on their own and that they are capable of being intertwined. Most Christians would of course maintain that the Scriptures provide the substance, the authority and the inspired guidelines for what God says to us, but silence and the ministry of teachers can be effective means of conveying and applying those basic principles.

Once again then, it's all gain? It could be, but once again the red lights flash here and there.

It is possible to idolize prophets and teachers. How easily. It is not only American televangelists who move the masses by their oratory or (at worst) their manipulative skill. Whenever a well-known speaker's name is mentioned with a catch in the breath he (or she) is being invested with more authority than is warranted. An idolized speaker can have an off day and produce platitudes and even heresies and the glassy-eyed congregation will drink in every word as if it came directly from God. Measure up your prophets and your gurus just as John called us to 'test the spirits to see whether they are from God, for many false prophets have gone out into the world' (1 John 4:1).

It is possible to idolize silence. While the silent mind and spirit can be wonderfully open to God's presence and to his communication, it is also easy to enjoy the feeling of peacefulness so that 'getting into silence' can become a merely pleasurable exercise. And God very often has uncomfortable things to say to us. If your silence is all comfort and passive delight, beware. Obviously there is a danger if we assume that every idea that comes to us in silence is from God. There are other beings looking for a blank mind to write on. So once again, silence can be a great boon, and to exercise appreciation of silence a healthy antidote to the panic of modern life, but measure up your silence and do not let it become central, where God belongs.

But surely it is not possible to idolize Scripture? Oh yes it is, as Jesus himself warned:

'You search the scriptures because you think that in them you have eternal life; and it is they that testify on my behalf. Yet you refuse to come to me to have life' (John 5:39–40).

Eternal life is to be found in Christ and him alone, not in the *words* of the Bible even if we know them all off by heart. Your fiancée's love letters may tell you a lot about her, but you can't marry a heap of paper.

Personality type

It may seem a little strange, perhaps even shocking, to lump together silent retreats and 'Gales Week'-type celebrations as if they were the same thing. Devotees of each often regard the others as being from another planet and not able to understand the same language. But the differences may be more superficial than fundamental.

Many readers, on seeing the heading 'personality type' will automatically mutter 'Myers-Briggs'. A recent fashion for Christians, as well as many others, has been the Myers-Briggs personality-type indicator tests, which label us with four initials and place us in boxes according to our expressed preferences. The first and most obvious distinction is between extrovert and introvert. The extrovert charges his/her energy batteries by getting together with others; the introvert gains strength from being alone. It would immediately seem likely that the extrovert will head for 'Gales Week', the introvert to Bradgate Abbey. Many other factors may influence the choice, but the point is that this is likely to be a personality-type choice not a spiritual one. Or it may be that you go where your group is going whether you like it or not.

These groups have more in common (wanting to leave the world for a time, to recharge failing spiritual batteries, to hear God speaking, to learn his way for them) than the different expressions of fellowship and devotion would suggest. There are pitfalls of idolatry in both extremes (and in the middle) but there are also great riches to be experienced.

Perhaps it should be remarked in passing that the Myers-Briggs system is generally descriptive and non-directive, but it is often suggested that we should not only go where our personality leads us but also push the barriers a little and make ourselves experience something that we may not expect to enjoy. So the extrovert should try a silent retreat (perhaps for a few hours, not beginning with an eight-day Ignatian variety) and the introvert should visit 'Gales Week' for a day. It may not be as difficult as you thought and you might learn something, not least that you are capable of a bit of adventure!

This chapter has been directed to those who have the time, the money and the inclination to get away occasionally. What about the rest of us who lack one or more of these commodities? We may be saying, 'If there are as many problems as all that it isn't worth the candle anyway.'

But the principles still apply, whether we use these facilities or not. Jesus still calls us to come away with him to a quiet place, even if it is only our own bathroom or the foot of a nearby tree. We all need to pause to hear him speaking to us; we all need the closeness of the fellowship of others to help us to worship. In fact the Christian who is able to find quiet and fellowship, to hear God speaking through the Bible interpreted by the experience of life and does not have to rely on retreats and conventions may well find fewer dangers of idolizing God.

For us all, the need for real fellowship with God and with each other is a first step back from the influence of the idol factory.

CHAPTER 5

Healing and the Binker factor

Enjoying fellowship with God is a step of faith. It is a moving away from using God as a means of getting things done and a step towards letting him do what *he* wants. It may be a faltering and tentative step, but it is a positive one. Another such step, which has been taken by increasing numbers of believers, is allowing God to heal them, be it physically, emotionally, mentally or spiritually.

The 'healing movement' (if it can be so called, for it is very diffuse) runs parallel to the desire for fellowship with God and can often be seen in the same contexts – rallies, conferences, healing centres, organizations devoted to healing, healing groups, healing services. A high proportion of our churches pay some attention to spiritual healing. This tide has been rising for at least the past hundred years and is now running strongly. Fifty years ago physical healing was an unusual emphasis in the normal church; today it is fairly commonplace. Why is this?

The plus and the minus

As already hinted there are positive and wholesome reasons for the rediscovery of healing. Chiefly, we have understood what was really obvious all the time, that Jesus was a healer. The emphasis is very strong in the gospels. In the very first chapter of Mark we are told of a man possessed by an evil spirit who was freed, Simon's mother-in-law healed of a fever and,

> That evening, at sundown, they brought to him all
> who were sick or possessed with demons. And the
> whole city was gathered around the door. And he
> cured many who were sick with various diseases
> (Mark 1:32–34).

Certainly his healing was intended as a sign, a picture of the complete wholeness which forgiveness and reconciliation would bring, but Jesus healed people because he loved them, not just as visual aids to advertise his campaign. In fact he frequently ordered people not to talk about what had happened. He longed for them to be whole, spiritually as well as physically.

So surely Jesus continues to want us to be healed. He loves us now, from his position at the right hand of the Father and where he actually prays for us (see *e.g.* Hebrews 1:3; 7:25). We need not despise the work of the medical professions, but neither do we rely on them as if they had absolute power in the realms of the physical while God is limited to spiritual matters. We realize too that you cannot draw a boundary between them.

Another positive aspect of the increase of healing has been the rediscovery of spiritual gifts, particularly in the last half-century. Again it is all in the Bible, but it used to be necessary to 'explain away' the references to gifts of healing by assuming that they were intended only for the times of the New Testament and that now we live in a new dispensation when such gifts have been withdrawn. This continues to be a bone of contention between 'charismatics' and all who acknowledge the validity of God's spiritual gifts, and 'dispensationalists' and all who see the gifts as superseded. The reader must decide on this question, but there is another element to the rediscovery of healing, closely linked to this one.

Christianity, in the West at least, has become less formal than of old. Religion is talked about, not shunned as a taboo subject (as sex or death used to be). There is more openness; people are more free in discussing their problems, and asking for prayer. People are more ready to touch one another, to shake hands, to embrace, to 'lay hands' on one another in prayer. All of this is viewed with increasing dismay by some and increasing delight by others. But the point is that there is a growing *warmth* and fellowship observable. More Christians are seen to be caring for one another. The support of a small group praying for one's problems and pains can be a wonderful experience.

The rediscovery of Jesus' role as healer, of the gifts of the Spirit and the caring fellowship of believers are all on the plus side of the balance-sheet. Are there any debits to mention? There must be. Perhaps we can find, without too much research, some other reasons for the growth in the interest in physical healing in the past century.

A glance around the magazine-racks of the news-agents or along the shelves of the drug-stores and chemists' shops will give us a clue. The Western world, led perhaps by the USA (but it is not limited to America), has apparently gone overboard on health care. Controversy rages around the proportion of the Gross National Product spent on health services. Doctors are overwhelmed (with patients as well as with red tape). If a visitor from four hundred years ago could see us now he might be forgiven for assuming that we are all hypochondriacs. 'How are you?' has become more than a greeting, though we are usually more anxious to tell our friend how *we* are than to discover the details of their condition.

Physical well-being has taken the place of spiritual well-being.

That is the short, sharp and perhaps nasty summary of the matter. The body has taken over from the soul. When Christians believed that this life was a 'vale of tears' to be endured somehow so that eternal bliss could ensue, bodily ailments were of smaller importance than they are now. In any case there was little you could do about pain except suffer it. Now two things have happened. Medical science has advanced so far in the control of pain and the curing of disease that we have come to put our faith in medicine to free us from ills, to assume that we have a right to freedom from discomfort, to take legal action against the doctors and hospitals if they fail to do what we want.

Parallel with this rise of medical science has been the decline of belief in heaven. If there is no heaven (or we can't be sure enough about it) then this world becomes far more important than it was. It's all there *is*. This body is the only one I shall ever have. (Paul, who argued brilliantly for the 'resurrection body' in 1 Corinthians 15, thought otherwise, but then Paul is old hat isn't he?) So I must protect it from every possible attack of pain and disease.

Health has become an obsession. Fitness is a way of life. Is it really surprising then that Christians find their own interpretation of all this in a renewed interest in healing? We too are infected by the disease of health-mania. The difference is that the world looks to pills, potions, surgery and laser beams. The church looks to those panaceas too and adds, sometimes tentatively, prayer and the laying-on-of-hands or anointing with oil.

So perhaps it should be said that the rediscovery of the ministry of healing has been a very positive and wholesome movement, while on the other hand, the current obsession with physical health for its own sake takes a great deal of the shine off the silverware.

The Binker factor

But does God heal anyway? Investigations into the 'assured results' of healing ministry never seem to decide the matter one way or the other. The faithful believe and the sceptics come up with an explanation that satisfies them. There has never been, and perhaps never can be, any cast-iron proof that God has healed anyone. It depends where you draw the boundary of proof. Even if an amputee grows two new legs the sceptic will have recourse to the argument that it is wonderful, yes, in that sense a miracle, yes, but we don't know that *God* did it. Perhaps it was an unusual, even unique, natural phenomenon which we cannot yet explain.

Christians will also want to emphasize the opposite, that when surgery or medicine heals, it is merely the means God uses. It is basically God who does the healing.

Others, concerned to preserve good relations with the medical world, suggest that God heals mind and spirit and even emotions, but leaves the bodily aspect to the Health Service.

To even the firmest of believers there remains the enormous question mark of *Why*? Why, if God heals A does he not heal B who seems to be in greater need? There are many well-authenticated examples of healing, which all but the hardened sceptic will accept (*e.g.* Jennifer Rees-Larcombe, *Unexpected Healing*, Hodder and Stoughton, 1991). Why then does God not do the same for others who are equally meritorious or equally humble, equally prayed-for and would make wonderful publicity for the Kingdom of God? Why indeed? Writer Adrian Plass has summed it all up by saying that we know two facts as certain: God heals, and God does not heal. More than that we cannot claim.

But we do know that Jesus Christ represents God's attitude towards mankind and that his attitude is one of love, and Jesus Christ healed people's bodies. He did not heal them all, and in the end they all died. Even Lazarus died. Twice. This is a mystery and must remain so this side of eternity, but it is a mystery with a golden glow on it – the glow of God's love in Christ.

It is in trying to achieve healing where God does not seem, at least for the moment, to be willing it, that we stumble across the 'Binker factor'.

Binker, you may recall, was Christopher Robin's own particular imaginary friend, immortalized by A. A. Milne in *Now we are Six* (Methuen, 1927).

> Binker – what I call him – is a secret of my own,
> And Binker is the reason why I never feel alone.
> Playing in the nursery, sitting on the stair,
> Whatever I am busy at, Binker will be there.
>   Oh, Daddy is clever, he's a clever sort of man,
>   And Mummy is the best since the world began,
>   And Nanny is Nanny and I call her Nan –
>   But they can't
>   See
>   Binker.

Binker can talk, but the little boy has to do it for him because Binker has a sore throat. Binker cries when the soap gets into (Christopher Robin's) eyes. Binker can eat chocolates, but Christopher has two and eats Binker's for him as his teeth are 'rather new'. Binker is a delightful example of God made in the image of man, or in this case a friend made in the image of a little boy.

Binker in action

Joe Bishop was an ordinary sort of guy; middle-aged, a formal church-goer, not particularly holy. He suffered badly from arthritis. His church announced a healing service and Joe's wife persuaded him to go. His arthritis was particularly bad that night and he was unable to concentrate on what was going on at all. In response to the preacher's invitation he tottered to his feet and was led to the front. Someone laid a hand on his shoulder, a warm glow suffused his whole body and his pain vanished and did not return.

This experience revolutionized Joe's outlook. It was as if he had new life. His experience dominated his thinking and filled his waking hours. He began to want above all things to share his new-found healing with others, not just to tell them about it but to make it possible for them to share the experience too.

So Joe made a list of all that had happened on that memorable night. There had been a congregation, soft music and a sermon. The sick had been asked to stand (except for someone in a wheel-chair and that person, he noticed, had not been healed — significant that). A right hand had been laid on his left shoulder and a short prayer had been said. He asked the person concerned for the words of the prayer as far as he could remember them and wrote them down.

This launched Joe on his career as a healer. He began to hold meetings in his home, then in church halls and later, even in public arenas. Always a congregation, soft music, a sermon, the standing at the front, the right hand on the left shoulder.

And it worked!

Many people got better from all sorts of illnesses, some at once and others after a long time. Many got better, but some did not. Now these were an embarrassment. Joe could not understand why they were not healed until he realized that something had been missed out; the wrong music, a left hand being used instead of the right, the wrong words being used in the prayer. Yet even when all these details were sorted out still some were not healed. It must be that the patients lacked faith. Joe had done everything correctly; God was no weaker than he had been so the sufferers were told that though they might not feel better or look better they really *were* better. All they had to do was to claim their healing. God was right. Joe's methods were right. So it must depend on the sufferer.

So it came about that a growing number of blind, crippled, diseased and pain-full people followed Joe and believed that they were healed. They believed very convincingly, though members of their families did not share their convictions. But they all loved Joe and honoured him for his work and did not want to let him down. And Joe didn't want to admit failure in case it undermined the faith of the next congregation. So they all pretended to be healed.

As far as healing was concerned, their god was Binker and they had to do it for him as he didn't seem to provide the healing they wanted.

We have seen Joes on TV or in the flesh or read about them in magazines. They are mostly well-intentioned, godly people, genuinely wanting to share their gifts and by no means manipulating their hearers. But to attract a crowd you need a reputation and a healer's reputation does not increase with the number of people who are not healed.

I am not arguing against divine healing (how could I?). I am not suggesting that healing is always imaginary or self-induced. But I am concerned that people should be so worried about physical healing that they put it at the top of their agenda and are so challenged by the circumstances of the meeting or service that they indulge in wishful thinking and pretend to be healed. When they are not.

Of course there is such a thing as faith and there are

instances of people who continue to exhibit symptoms for a time but who steadfastly believe they will go – and they do. But there are others who believe equally steadfastly, nay desperately, and the symptoms remain. And too often the faith departs because it was based on the hope of a cure, rather than on the fatherhood of God, the saving grace of Christ and the loving presence of the Holy Spirit.

Supernatural health service

Once again there is not a clear yes or no answer to the question of healing. In opening ourselves to what God wants for us, without making selfish demands, we are putting ourselves at the disposal of Jesus the healer. God reserves his judgment and does what he wants. We cannot demand that he heals in every case and we must not pretend that he will. Sometimes Jesus was *unable* to heal (as in Capernaum where he found little faith). Sometimes he healed where faith was exercised by others, not the sick person (the paralytic lowered through the roof).

So, we should pray for healing, hope for it, delight in it when it happens but beware of using God as a means to our material comfort, a kind of free, supernatural health service.

Once again we find ourselves with a very slippery question: How can we know when we are moving from faith to selfish demand? Where is the boundary? And surely all our faith is mixed with greed and selfishness anyway. We just are not perfect. We cannot escape from the likelihood of trying to use God to some extent. Perhaps a closer examination of prayer will help us to disentangle some of this muddle.

CHAPTER 6

Intercession: 'Whatever you ask'?

Many good people have been so daunted by the problems of whether God answers prayer, how he answers it and whether it is morally right to ask for things at all (the danger of 'using God') that they have given up interceding altogether. Some have given up because of laziness or lack of commitment; others on principle that it must be wrong. God doesn't need our prayers and we can never know exactly what he wants us to pray for, so let's leave it at that.

The Bible does not lend support to that line. It is crammed full of people's prayers and encouragement to pray for things. 'Then Jesus told them a parable about their need to pray always and not to lose heart' (Luke 18:1). He told the disciples about a helpless widow who kept coming back to the judge, repeatedly asking for justice until she got it. Don't give up.

Three times a day Daniel would 'get down on his knees to pray to his God and praise him ... seeking mercy before his God' (Daniel 6:10–11).

The final flourish of Paul's great catalogue of spiritual armour is, 'Pray in the Spirit at all times in every prayer and supplication. To that end keep alert and always persevere in supplication for all the saints' (Ephesians 6:18).

Prayer is the vital breath of the church. The church (and the Christian) which stops praying stops living. Our slide into decay will not be halted but rather accelerated if we stop praying. But as we have already seen, it is the attitude with which we come to pray that matters. Whether we treat God with reverence or with arrogance makes all the difference.

Prayer: for whose benefit?

'Prayer' is a very wide-ranging word. It can mean intercession, worship, praise, adoration, confession, meditation, contemplation, supplication, thanksgiving or even 'groans that words cannot express' (Romans 8:26). Now this is becoming confusing. All this analysis could easily snuff out the real thing altogether and certainly promote yawns rather than cries for divine help. So let's ask one question: 'When I pray whom do I expect will benefit?' or perhaps, 'Who am I doing it for?' – for God? for me? for the people I'm praying for? Probably a bit of all three, but let us separate them out into those three categories.

The idea that I am praying for God's benefit may seem a little shocking. As we saw above, God doesn't *need* our prayers. He knows what we have need of before we ask him and we cannot add to God's stature by our prayer. If we think of God as needing our praise and worship it sounds as if he is a complacent and tyrannical ruler, living off the fawning flattery of his slaves – a very unpleasant picture and a million miles from the God of love. This brings us to the whole area of the validity of worship which is worth a chapter on its own, so we shall postpone discussion of it until then. If you can't wait, turn to page 61 but come back here later.

So what about prayer for *my* benefit (not, strictly speaking, intercession, which is prayer for others)? Many Christians instinctively feel that they should do nothing for their own benefit but do everything for others. Prayer for my benefit would be selfish, and selfishness is sin. But even these noble, stoical folk would have to agree that praying has done them good, even if it is only a spin-off. If you praise God and intercede for others you do feel better for it. And surely even they will not be too proud to call upon God 'in the day of trouble' (Psalm 50:15). It is our instinct. 'Prayer is the soul's sincere desire, uttered or unexpressed' (James Montgomery).

But quite apart from not wanting to be selfish, prayer is our meeting with God. Is it selfish to wish to enjoy the presence of God? Is it selfish for a child to wish to be in the company of its father or mother? This aspect of prayer as fellowship with God has received well-deserved publicity in recent years. Prayer is no longer seen basically as a chore, repeating a shopping list of requests before a stony-faced God who has to be persuaded to respond by the degree of our earnestness or the sheer quantity of our prayers. In fact Isaiah told us that millennia ago, passing on to us the words of God, 'even though you make many prayers, I will not listen' (Isaiah 1:15). This almost mechanistic approach to prayer comes clearly under the heading of idolatry, the very problem we keep stumbling upon – trying to persuade God to do what we think best by our efforts.

So a move towards spending time in fellowship with God, learning to know him better, enjoying his presence, being still and knowing that he is God (even if the much loved Psalm 46:10 probably means 'Stop fighting and I will fight for you'), all this is healthy and is clearly what God wants of us – that we speak to him and he to us and that we live close to him.

But as soon as we have said that, we can see the danger of moving off into idolatry in the opposite direction. 'Resting in the Lord's presence' so easily suggests a feeling of peacefulness. The word 'peace' (really meaning 'shalom', a new, wholesome and vibrant relationship) conjures up pictures of sunsets and green meadows with cows quietly chewing – bliss – nirvana ... we are well on the way to the Buddhist idea of 'heaven', an absorption into the divine nothingness (if this is unfair to Buddhism, I apologize; it is very near to some 'Christianity' that I have met). We met this escapism in chapter four. This is the danger of prayer being almost entirely for my benefit and that benefit being seen as a feeling of rosy comfortableness. Is it surprising that people can get the same feelings from Yoga or from merely sitting in the sun by a fish pond? Is this necessarily the presence of God? It may be, but is this all that God has in store for us? Have we 'succeeded' in prayer only if we feel a miasmic glow? I very much doubt it.

Prayer is very beneficial if it brings us close to God, but God is not a cosy for our afternoon teapot. We may get too close if we are not careful, like the people of Israel at Mount Sinai, who were ordered to stand back lest God 'break out' on them (see Exodus 19). This is not the comfortable God we have learned to love at our mother's knee, but it is the God of the Old Testament. We do well not to take too much for granted. 'It is a fearful thing to fall into the hands of the living God.' And that's in the *New* Testament (Hebrews 10:£1). It has been well said that God comforts the disturbed and disturbs the comfortable. Both truths need to be held simultaneously.

Make your requests known

The third beneficiary of our prayers will be the people for whom we are praying. We leave aside now the elements of confession and worship, and the element of fellowship with God, and focus on the work of prayer as intercession, asking for things on behalf of others as well as ourselves. This is where using God as an idol can emerge in its clearest form. We are told that we must pray and that God will use our prayers, and when we do just that we are accused of using God as a means of getting our will done. Then when we pray 'but your will be done', people accuse us of lack of faith and they say the prayer of faith is the only prayer that will be answered (Matthew 21:21–22 and James 1:6–8 for instance). *Does* our prayer change things?

As a child I was not very interested in church. It was stuffy and boring. Need I go further? But I was interested in God. 'Pious young upstart,' you say. No, by no means, 'Selfish young materialist' would be nearer the mark. God was useful. I had two particular fears as a small child, at least there are two that I remember vividly: fear of thunderstorms and of stomach-ache. Both seemed to occur frequently (perhaps the latter was brought on by the former; I don't think it could have been the other way round) and there seemed to be no way of escaping them except prayer. So I prayed most earnestly to be delivered from pains in the interior (perhaps I should have been more concerned with my diet) and that God would send the thunderclouds elsewhere (my love for my fellow-creatures was minimal).

I have a typical memory of a stiflingly hot summer day, airless and still, the leaves on the trees making only an occasional feeble signal that wind would ever come again. Then, around tea-time, the sun disappeared behind a purple cloud, edged with brilliant gold, and the whole western sky seemed to be enveloped in a pall of gloom. A hot wind got up – from the east – wonderful! But the hard-edged cloud came inexorably on, getting blacker by the minute and already dull rumbles of approaching thunder could be heard. I fled in panic to my bedroom and knelt by the bed. 'Please God, *please* take away the thunderstorm', over and over again. Where that thunderstorm went I shall never know. It seemed absolutely inevitable that it would break over our heads and that we should be dashed to bits by forked lightning, thunderbolts and a deluge such as last seen in the days of Noah. But no, it quietly passed by, with perhaps a shower of rain, and God had answered my prayer.

Now had he? Certainly I fulfilled Hallesby's condition of helplessness. But surely I didn't move God to change the weather! It was a purely selfish prayer. I didn't care if people in Coventry or Shrewsbury or Derby were inundated. It was a clear case of idolatry, trying to use God to gain my own ends. But as far as I was concerned it worked. No matter that it never seems to have worked again since and that it doesn't work for millions who live in fear of far greater disasters in equatorial zones. But that answer to my prayer, which many people will dismiss as a convenient coincidence, began to lead me to God, to begin to grow up in my praying but not to doubt that God was there.

All of this seems to be quite contrary to what I want to argue, that God will not tolerate being used as a slot-machine. But in honesty I have to record it because it is an exception to my rule and God does not work by my rules. Whenever we describe the boundaries of God's activity we are, as it were, inviting him to show us where we are wrong. He has no boundaries. 'For as the heavens are higher than the earth, so are my ways higher than your ways' declares the Lord (Isaiah 55:9). God may do the impossible for the benefit of a small frightened child, but as we grow more mature we need to co-operate with him rather than merely beat on his door with our little fists.

What happens when we pray? Does God alter events on our behalf? It seems so sometimes and we must be content to thank him when we see it happening. I hope

I was duly thankful to God for the passing of the storm. Certainly in later years Beethoven's hymn of thanksgiving after the storm in his Pastoral Symphony has had a special meaning for me. I am grateful too that he has removed much of my fear of thunderstorms. But we can never know that God has altered events because we can know only what has happened. We can never know what would have happened if . . . because it didn't. So we have to rest ignorant and perhaps not content but leave the question open. God only knows whether he changes events or not. So let's be positive and ask what is a mature approach to intercession.

Completing the circle

Praying for my own needs of course was not intercession. Intercession is praying on behalf of others, but I used the illustration because it was vivid in my experience and the principle can be applied broadly.

We don't know whether God will change circumstances as a result of our intercessions, but we must pray *as if he will*. This is surely the only way to approach the subject. In chapter two we looked at the first of O. Hallesby's basic principles of true prayer – helplessness. Perhaps God encourages the little child and the new convert with wonderful answers to their prayers precisely because they are helpless and are in need of such encouragement lest the faltering flame of their faith goes out altogether. The second principle which Hallesby points to is faith.

As the author points out, the very mention of the need for faith in our intercession is enough to dry up our prayer at once. Do I have to believe absolutely that what I pray for will happen? If I don't have enough faith, will God not be willing to help? Is it my faith that is achieving the answer to my prayer then, or God's power? If it depends on me I'd better give up at once, because I shall be using God as an idol again.

> When an honest soul examines himself in the light of the Scriptures, he soon finds that faith is just what seems lacking in his prayers. It says that he should ask in faith, nothing doubting. He does just the opposite. He doubts before he prays, while he prays, and after he has prayed. He is just like the surge of the sea; he is driven and tossed to and fro by the winds of doubt. He is the very man whom Scripture depicts: 'a doubleminded man, unstable in all his ways'.
>
> (O. Hallesby, *Prayer*, p. 23)

But the author goes on to point out that things are not half as bad as we thought. The very fact of our helplessness is the first requirement of true prayer, and the fact that we recognize it and bring it to the feet of Christ is the second. For faith is not a cast-iron certainty that our will shall be done, but a humble request that God's will shall be done. 'If it is your will' is not an improper, faithless hedging of our bets. Jesus used the phrase himself in Gethsemane. Sometimes we may have the gift of faith which makes God's will clear to us and all of us know from the Bible what kind of things God requires, but we rarely know exactly what he wants. We can but co-operate with him to the best of our knowledge. Let Hallesby bring us some encouragement:

> We need not exert ourselves and try to force ourselves to believe, or try to chase doubt out of our hearts. Both are just as useless. It begins to dawn on us that we can bring everything to Jesus, no matter how difficult it is; and we need not be

frightened away by our doubts or our weak faith, but only tell Jesus how weak our faith is. We have let Jesus into our hearts, and He will fulfill our hearts' desires.

(O. Hallesby, Prayer, p. 28)

All true prayer is finding out what God's will is and then co-operating with him in the doing of it. True prayer then originates with God, purposes to accomplish his will and thus returns glory to God. But there is a gap in the circle. For some obscure reason God has left that gap for us to fill. Our prayers are needed, we know not why, to complete the circle. We do not claim credit for initiating the prayer. We do not accomplish the task, but we are needed to make the connection.

Someone has said that God graciously allows us to participate in what he is doing. He holds our hand as we try to draw his picture, and, if we will let him, makes the picture for us. (This illustration is a theological one and is not meant for teachers of art, who will be horrified!)

Christina Baxter (St John's College, Nottingham) has defined intercession as, 'The prayer of Jesus to the Father on the lips of the believer, by the power of the Holy Spirit.' If we, as believers, are privileged to take part in an activity which is going on at that kind of level nothing more profound can be said.

CHAPTER 7

A spot of worship

In the last two chapters we have looked at prayer which was primarily intended for our own upbuilding (meditation, contemplation, listening to God) and prayer for the benefit of others (intercession). We touched on, and now return to, prayer which is intended to glorify God: worship and praise. This may well include thanksgiving. At its best it will be our natural reaction to God, not a calculated decision that 'God wants my worship, therefore I'd better do some.'

Definitions

There have been many definitions of worship. The word may have already suggested to some a specific section of a service in church, or perhaps even before the service proper begins, which entails the singing of worship songs. We shall come back to this presently. Others understand worship as performing a prescribed rite from a prayer book, 'holding a service'. Others will see it in the light of our old friend the sunset when they can 'feel the glory of God'. Let me give you my working definition so that you can at least know what you are disagreeing with!

Worship is our appropriate response to what we realize to be the 'worthship' of God.

1. By 'appropriate response' I do not mean to refer only to private worship (the sunset) nor only to corporate worship of the group together (whether

structured or spontaneous, tight-lipped or hilarious). All of this may well be included in worship. But it also covers our whole way of life: 24 hours a day, 168 hours a week, not just from 10.30 to 12.00 on a Sunday morning (or whenever it is) and not just when we read the Bible or pray. Worship is a way of life. The apostle Paul made just this point when he wrote to the church in Rome:

> I appeal to you therefore, brothers and sisters, by the mercies of God, to present your bodies as a living sacrifice, holy and acceptable to God, *which is your spiritual worship* (Romans 12:1, italics mine).

2. The reason that worship means much more than just going through certain motions or experiencing certain feelings can be found in the second phrase of my definition, 'what we realize'. This means both in the usual sense 'come to understand' and also in the original sense 'come to make real' or 'act upon'. If it hits us who God really is or what Jesus has really done for us; if, in other words, we have a sudden clear view of the nature of God, our proper reaction will be to fall down before him in wonder, love and praise. But it will go well beyond that. We shall want to show by our lives that we have taken on board who God really is and so we shall want our attitudes, and our habits of thought even, to fall into line with the will of this God whom we have come fully to recognize. As Paul wrote in the second verse of the chapter quoted above:

> Do not be conformed to this world, but be trans- formed by the renewing of your minds, so that you may discern what is the will of God – what is good and acceptable and perfect.

Our response of worship is to bow down or kneel before God and to align the rest of our life with his will. As we do so, we open ourselves to the way that he wants us to live and are better able to assess what he wants. As we obey, we will want to worship more truly and the whole very rich and wholesome cycle starts all over again.

3. The 'worthship of God'. Much has been made of the derivation of our word 'worship' from the Old English word *weorthscipe*. Not every scholar now agrees about the details, but in any case it provides a helpful clue to understanding. It is God's worth that we are properly reacting to, not his command ('Bow down or I will throw you into a furnace', which was King Nebuchadnezzar's approach in Daniel 3), nor his emotive pleading, nor yet his reasoned argument. The Bible gives us a clear picture of who God is and what he is like and we are left with the decision, 'What shall I do about it, seeing that God is like that?' If I do nothing I am still answering the question. If my heart and mind and will are all (in some proportion) affected by God's mercy, as Paul wrote, I shall respond appropriately only by worshipping him in spirit and in truth, including action. My immediate thought was not to please God – I was just responding to reality as I saw it – but Paul assures us that our holiness, our living as God wants us to, *is* pleasing to God.

It will also be very satisfying to us, and we should be careful not to suspect worship for this reason. If we stopped doing everything that gave us any pleasure we should be perverting God's good intentions for us (1 Timothy 6:17, end of verse). We should also die from the lack of progeny but before that from starvation! No, we should thank God that doing things his way results in great satisfaction and joy for us. It is at this point that the danger of idolatry presents itself, even as a small cloud on the horizon.

'Worship does you good'

There seems nothing wrong with singing worship songs together (always assuming that God is the subject of our worship; we are not only enjoying the music or sharing an activity). You can call the activity a 'worship spot' and not offend any of God's laws. But when people urge us to 'try a spot of worship' to help us over depression, or announce a 'spot of worship' to get us into the mood (the mood for what?), red lights begin to flash. The old enemy, using God to promote a feeling of pleasure, is upon us.

We cannot object to someone *enjoying* a church service either. One of the aspects of church life most satirized by non-churchgoers (and many churchgoers too) is the dullness and gloom of church services. This is changing now and is by no means as bad as it was fifty years ago. So if people enjoy services: great! But have you not heard this kind of thing:

'O Vicar, I *have* enjoyed this little service. It gives me a little lift, you know, every time I come. And I think that every time God sees me sitting here he gives me a little smile and I know that he doesn't mind about my little shortcomings during the week. I don't know what I should do without it. I have been coming here for 57 years now and I so look forward to sitting in my little pew and seeing the little choir boys. You know, Mr Bush was a choirboy once . . .' and so on. Apart from the fact that everything (including God?) is little, this person has not advanced beyond using the service as a weekly security, using not even God but the church building and what happens there as a crutch. Before we sneer at such people we might remember that one-legged folk *need* crutches and we do not know how they came to lose the other leg. Without judging them too harshly, however, we have to say that this kind of 'worship' is immature and should be encouraged to deepen.

So true worship and praise is another step away from the idolatry of God but, like everything else, it too can degenerate into self-centred pleasure-seeking. Or we may hope to placate God, to buy him off by attending to a duty that we hope will please him. Before we leave this subject, however, perhaps we can uncover a little more of the contrast between duty and emotional feelings. Is it just that some of us are so constructed that duty is as far as we shall ever get, while others, naturally emotional, cannot progress beyond feelings?

Duty

As a young Christian I was conscripted into the Royal Air Force for my statutory two years of National Service. I determined to behave in as Christlike a manner as possible and so to be a witness in 'the hut'. I had no difficulty with reading the Bible in public or even praying. In fact the other men seemed to respect these odd habits and sometimes apologized to me for swearing. One problem, however, remained a problem: what I felt like when I woke up in the morning.

Sleep may carry one into fearsome places or delightful ones. Sweet dreams may be a blessing, but to awaken from them can be a nasty shock. At the time in question the School of Administrative Training, RAF Credenhill, Hereford, had installed a tannoy system which broadcast every morning at (I think it was) 6.30 am very loudly, 'Good morning, good morning, we've danced the whole night through. Good morning, good morning to you!' Was it Frank Sinatra? I don't wish to remember. When this deafening cacophony had finally blown itself out, the airman in the bed opposite mine would sit up and make his ritual pronouncement, 'I *hate* the RAF!' He said it with great regularity and great venom. It was not a positive start to the day.

Now I had intended to begin every morning with worship. Not that I was uninhibited or tactless enough to sing, you understand, but I meant to begin by repeating to myself the opening of that hymn, 'When morning gilds the skies, my heart awaking cries, "May Jesus Christ be praised".' The idea was good, but the feeling with which I staggered down the concrete passageway with my safety razor and shaving cream was a mixture of, 'When morning gilds the skies, we've danced the whole night through, my heart awaking cries, "I *hate* the RAF".' Jesus Christ was not always praised. Or perhaps he was; who knows?

The point I should like to make is that I was given grace to press on and say through my teeth (which were often chattering – it was November/December) 'May Jesus Christ be praised' even though my heart was not responding. Worship is the appropriate response to what we realize about God. But what if my awaking heart does *not* cry, 'May Jesus Christ be praised'? Must he go unpraised just because I don't feel like it? Is worship so spontaneous that I can do it only when I'm in the mood for it? That may not happen very often. No, surely one aspect of worship, like love, is that it is an act of the will – a decision taken in view of what we know of the reality of God, to say certain things, to do certain things, to respond as best we can to God's love. Is worship then a duty? The answer is, 'Yes'.

Feelings

I can almost hear the cries of dismay which greet this conclusion. 'If that is all there is to worship you have confirmed what we suspected of you. You are a dry-as-dust old stick-in-the-mud, probably Anglican, with no spontaneity, no joy and, dare we say it, no Holy Spirit in sight.'

I will not answer the charge point by point, but I certainly didn't say that duty was *all* there is to worship. What I stand by is that it is an appropriate response to God's love for me to worship him in will and in deed *whether I feel like it or not*.

But worship is also a function of the emotions. Of course it is. Whether you approach God through candle flames, incense and motets by Byrd or Palestrina; or through butterflies and garden flowers; or through worship songs, raised hands and cries of 'Praise you, Lord!', real worship must have its source in the real God as revealed in Scripture and we shall be moved in our own way to express our appreciation.

'In our own way.' Let's face it, some of us are cold fishes (and need to be warmed up a bit!); others are 'on fire' (and need a dose of silence now and then), but gratitude and thankfulness for what God has done for us in creation and in Christ's life, death and resurrection on our behalf must surely produce some feeling. Or perhaps we need to pray for the ability to grasp the truth. Once we do, some feelings must be stirred.

Yes, worship is certainly a matter of emotion, both in the corporate expression of praise in music, prayer or dance, and in the daily living when we can occasionally thank God for his goodness.

So is that it? Worship is a duty; worship is feeling? If that were the whole story there would still be that spectre of idolatry creeping in. Worship as a duty can degenerate into trying to please God so as to buy favours from him. Perhaps he'll let me off if I do enough worshipping. Worship as feeling can very easily sink into doing it purely for our own enjoyment and assuming that God is enjoying it too. Are we sure that his taste in music is identical with ours? Surely there must be something beyond duty and feelings.

Relationship

In fact true worship must be more than either, or both put together. Duty is the response of the will to what we are convinced of in our minds. We *ought*. Feelings are the response of the emotions to what is happening. We *enjoy* or we are awestruck. But these are different ways of response, not the essence of worship itself. That essence is relationship. Worship is the response of a person to another Person: God.

A child may frequently go shopping for his mother. He may do it because he is ordered to and he sees it as his duty to obey. He may do it, on the other hand, because he enjoys shopping (though not many boys do). The best and basic reason for the shopping, however, is that he loves his mother. It is his response to their relationship. He knows that it is what she wants and he's glad to do it. Duty and enjoyment may be present too, either together or by turns, but love is the mainspring.

So it should be with worship. We worship God in prayer, song, heart and deed because we respond with gratitude to his love. What matters to the worshippers is not whether they are fulfilling a duty, nor whether they will enjoy it, but whether they are responding to God – not themselves. God is central. The idol is fallen.

CHAPTER 8

Guidance

The bowler-hatted young businessman walks briskly down the High Street towards the station. When he reaches the telephone box he pauses, waits for a space in the traffic and crosses the street. After walking twenty yards on the opposite side he crosses back again and disappears into the station. There's nothing very interesting about this perhaps, except that the following morning the same thing happens. And he does it again on Wednesday. The newspaper seller, who sits at the station entrance, is watching, fascinated. On Thursday morning, when the young man repeats his performance (and nearly loses his life in the process) the stall-holder asks him why he does it. 'Oh,' says the businessman, reddening, 'the Lord has told me to.'

'But why?'

'I don't know. Perhaps I shall be preserved from an accident one day. Perhaps a bus will mount the pavement where I would have been if I hadn't crossed. Good morning.'

You certainly see life when you're selling newspapers.

Does God have his hand on your shoulder?

That young man may be an extreme example. One hears of people wearing odd socks or leaving the dishes unwashed 'because the Lord told me to'. But well back from the lunatic-fringe there are many thousands, probably millions of Christians who are deeply concerned to do exactly what God tells them to do. They 'hear' his voice (often as an inner conviction rather than in audible words) and may well be glad to tell others about it. There are many millions more Christians who do not claim to hear God speaking to them but believe that he has his hand firmly on their shoulder and that he will indicate which way they should go, in matters great and small. One of the classic Bible verses on this is Isaiah 30:21:

> And when you turn to the right or when you turn
> to the left, your ears shall hear a word behind you,
> saying, 'This is the way; walk in it.'

It's significant that the words that follow are, 'Then you will defile your silver-covered idols and your gold-plated images. You will scatter them like filthy rags . . .' (Isaiah 30:22). If God is guiding us there is no place for an idol on the shelf.

In this what we may call the 'classic' Christian view of guidance, at least in this century, it is assumed that God has an ideal plan for each of our lives, from beginning to end. In theory, if we are ready and able to use all the means of guidance which God has given us, we shall hear his voice at every turn, obey it and find ourselves constantly in the centre of his will, doing always what is best.

It follows that every time we are disobedient to God's voice or every time we fail to listen in the right way we miss the ideal and fall short of God's plan. It may be that if we repent the ideal pattern can be restored, but it may also be that a wrong turning early on might lead to 'second-best' or 'third-best' lives. Many conscientious Christians have lived under the cloud of what they see as having missed God's best at a crucial time in their past and are paying the penalty.

On the other hand, a firm belief in God's daily guidance and his hand upon our major decisions means that the ultimate responsibility for running our lives is with God and not with us and this is a great relief. If I have honestly made my best decision before the Lord (we will think about this in more detail presently), I can leave the outcome with him and need not be anxious about it

This kind of thinking is much too difficult for many good Christians to swallow. How could the creator of the galaxies possibly be interested in the details of my life? they ask. In theory the answer to that is easy. The creator of the universe is also the creator of the atom. If nothing is too big for him, nothing is too small either. He can even pay attention to all of us at once. ('How many phone lines has he?' asked the small boy.) These are rather immature questions when asked like this, but they do cloak a very real fear in the minds of people who cannot bring themselves to feel that God can be concerned with them as individuals. They accept his creation and his salvation ('Jesus died for us all and I am one of those'), but not his daily involvement with them, except as a sort of general providence.

Then look at all the guilt these 'guided' people get involved in when they miss the way. You've just admitted that.

In any case, surely God wants us to grow up into adulthood and not remain childishly dependent on his every whim all our lives. What kind of children should we be bringing up if we told them what to do every minute of the day? They'd never grow up at all!

So one section of the Christian church asks God for guidance and believes that it is received. Another section does not believe that God wants to guide at all and so never asks for it (except perhaps in an emergency –

well, we're all human), but seems to manage reasonably well. How can we resolve this question? Is it just a matter of temperament? And where does it get us in our discussion of idolatry?

Principles

I have given an unfair caricature of both extremes, so it's only reasonable to look at the matter more seriously.

There can be no doubt that most Christians have believed that God can and does have a personal interest in them.

> For it was you who formed my inward parts;
>> you knit me together in my mother's womb ...
> Your eyes beheld my unformed substance.
> In your book were written
>> all the days that were formed for me,
>> when none of them as yet existed.
>> (Psalm 139:13, 16)

That was David's impression. And if Christ cared enough to die for humanity in general that means you and me in particular, and he will not leave us without help on a daily basis. The Bible and church history and hymnody are full of it. So how do I know what God wants me to do?

1. *The Bible.* He will not want me to do anything that negates the clear teaching of the Bible. The Commandments are basic principles. However clearly I may hear an inner voice telling me to keep something I have borrowed, 'Thou shalt not steal' is paramount. However 'right' it may seem for me to sleep with my neighbour's wife, 'Thou shalt not commit adultery' remains absolute. This is the negative value of the Bible. It defines what we are not guided to do.

The positive value is that it tells us what we *are* guided to be: loving, joyful, peaceful and so on (Galatians 5:21–22). Problems arise, however, when we try to use the Bible for specific guidance. Sometimes God will use a verse, a passage, a word even, to speak to us, but because it can happen it does not mean that it always will. To open the Bible at random may occasionally produce just the direction we needed. But it is not guaranteed, and may easily degenerate into superstition. There is no better warning against this practice than the unfortunate who turned up 'Judas went and hanged himself', decided to try again and landed on 'Go and do thou likewise.' Sometimes the story continues with a third despairing attempt which produced, 'What thou doest, do quickly.' It's an old story, as the King James version may suggest. Perhaps it shows that God has a sense of humour. We shall consider using the Bible to obtain what we want presently, but let us say now that we need to read it carefully, prayerfully and humbly if we are to hear the Lord's direction, and we need to be ready to obey what we are sure of.

2. *Our gifts.* It is unusual for God to call us to do something we are not fitted for. Occasionally he does, and he is able to equip us if he so decides, but normally we should expect him to use our already existing gifts and develop them. Nor does he necessarily call us to do what we dislike. The idea that we shall know what God wants because it is what we least want, betrays a dismal view of God. Paul reminded the Philippians that God called them both to will and to do his good pleasure (2:13), not just to obey but to enjoy it and to want it.

3. *Circumstances.* Again God may make it clear that we are to defy circumstances. Gladys Aylward, missionary to China, turned down by the China Inland Mission, set off to find her way to China on her own. Mad

English lady! Perhaps. God used *her* madness to great effect. But most of us would take it that God had closed that door and would pick some others. We can often see the hand of God in what he makes impossible or very difficult.

4. *Prayer and listening.* We come to recognize God's call more clearly as we get to know him better. To presume upon his guidance without being willing to listen is arrogance. Even then we need to be careful what we 'hear'. Not every inner voice is from God.

5. *Advice.* The prayerful advice of friends is always of great value. It is never to be absolutely decisive. Paul was advised strongly by experienced Christians, prophets included, not to go to Jerusalem, but believed that the Holy Spirit was leading him there.

6. *'Fleeces'.* This one is not to be generally recommended but it worked for Gideon (Judges 6). Unsure whether God wanted him to go and fight the Midianites and the Amalekites he prayed that if he put out a dry fleece it would be wet with dew while the ground around it remained dry. When this happened he tried a harder one. He asked God to make the fleece dry and the ground wet! It worked again so he could find no further grounds for doubt. God *may* wish to use this method with you – some people can tell you how it happened for them, but just because Gideon tried it does not mean that we all should. It sounds ominously like idolatry to me, but let each person be persuaded in his/her mind.

7. *Conscience.* This is another notoriously difficult area. It worked for Pinocchio: 'Give a little whistle, and always let your conscience be your guide.' But our Jiminy Crickets are not all reliable. Conscience can be stifled. However, it is fair to say that if your conscience is really troubling you over a decision you are making, be careful. As the old flag-signal used at sea indicated,

'You are standing into danger.' Be very sure that you are right before you disobey conscience.

8. *Church authority.* Some churches give no help to individuals or families anxious to know what to do. Others are far too directive and even manipulative. You are fortunate if you have a church which has a wise sense of discipline and responsibility and has the structure for helping you to discern God's will for you.

9. *Experience.* The more we listen to God and receive his guidance, the better we shall be at recognizing what he wants us to do. When one door closes, another opens – or perhaps a window. Yet even the greatest saints have had to walk in darkness and know the apparent absence of God. Sometimes he does seem to leave us without guidance. And it is then, when we have considered all the ingredients and principles outlined here, that we have to say, 'Lord, I am stepping into the dark. The way is not clear, but this seems to be the best alternative, so I'm going to do it. If I'm wrong, please intervene and stop me.' And in that faith we can step forward and may well find that he had his hand on us all the time.

Playing the guidance game

As I have said earlier, if we approach the subject (and approach God) humbly and thoughtfully these principles can be of help. They are not watertight and cannot be guaranteed to come up with the goods every time, but many Christians have reason to thank God for showing them just enough light to see by; the next step along the road.

Human nature is amazingly versatile, however, and our minds are crooked beyond belief. Without realizing it we can hear the guidance that we *want* to hear, persuade ourselves that black is white and white is black and can 'receive' not God's guidance but a reflection of our own intentions. And believe me, a person who is confused and humbly uncertain of God's will for them is far less dangerous than someone who is certain of God's guidance. And *wrong*.

At a crudely simple level we might decide what we want to do, say a prayer over the plan, 'O God bless my plan', and then believe that God has told us to do it. But wait a minute. That is exactly what very often does happen. When we had decisions to make about what job to apply for, where to live, what church to join, and most importantly, whether we should marry or not, my girl-friend, then fiancée, now wife, and I used to pray together and write lists of pros and cons and go through all the hoops which I have described. After some years she said, 'I don't think we ought to pray for guidance anymore. Because God always seems to guide *us* the way *you* want to go.' Ho hum.

Adrian Plass has brilliantly exposed the dangers of expecting God's guidance in stereotyped ways. One remembers his conviction that God wanted him to buy a Volvo and how he was astonished at the large number of Volvos he kept seeing . . .

Each of the nine principles can be used, just as an idol can be used, to provide us with the answer we want. Suppose I want, deep down, perhaps without knowing it, to live overseas. I frequently encounter Bible verses like, 'Go therefore and make disciples of all nations' (Matthew 28:19). Of course. Because my mind filters out verses like 'Return to your home, and declare how much God has done for you' (Luke 8:39). A subconscious switch illuminates one verse and darkens the other.

It is not difficult to persuade ourselves that we have the gifts we need in order to be an overseas missionary. And the more spiritual among us will express faith that God will gift us as necessary so there's no need for them yet. Circumstances may be against us, but they are the devil's attempt to prevent us from doing God's will. We must overcome them.

In prayer we shall be likely to hear the loudest voice telling us what to do and that voice may be our own. God's 'still small voice' (1 Kings 19:12, 'a gentle whisper' in NIV) may be easily drowned. The advice of our friends may be mistaken; we may decide that our church has no right to dictate to us. 'Fleeces' are notoriously unreliable and our consciences are by this time so confused that they sink without trace. Playing the guidance game can be just as idolatrous as following the stars on page whatever-it-is in the tabloid press. Guidance is really available if we will approach the Lord in the right spirit, but using the technique without really wanting to come close to God in the first place is worse than useless and contributes to the sum total of 'God-using' which we are trying to break free from.

But perhaps you are genuinely sincere. You have a big decision to make. You are pulled in all directions by Bible verses, advice and all the principles of guidance. You have read books on guidance. Your conscience needle is swinging round and round like a magnetic compass in an ironmonger's shop. You are as humble as can be and genuinely long to know God's will and *yet* the heavens remain as brass and you cannot see an inch before you, let alone a whole step.

At this point you need to stand back from yourself. You really have done all you can. It's about time you left it to God to manage. He can cope with your life without your turning your conscience inside out. Weigh the matter up just once more. Pray it over once more with a friend, if you are fortunate enough to have a praying friend, put your hand into the hand of God and just go. He won't let you fall.

CHAPTER 9

'Did God say?'

The Bible continues to be an international best-seller. Millions of copies are bought each year. What are they used for? A white one sometimes adorns a radiant bride in her wedding video. Big black ones sometimes impress the impressionable in solemn gatherings. Huge gilt-edged ones are borne aloft on the wings of gold eagles in ornate churches. A copy may be carried in procession and kissed by a priest; a copy may be used to prop up a projector . . .

In former days the Bible was treated with respect and reverence and would certainly never have propped up projectors even if they had been around. There is a story told of a child who found herself alone and marooned on the Longships lighthouse off the coast of Land's End, Cornwall, in 1795. Even today the Carn Bras rocks on which the pencil of a building rests are much better viewed from the cliffs than at close quarters. In stormy weather, which is frequent, the waves are terrible to behold. In previous centuries, with no comfort of helicopters to come to the rescue and with the thunder of the seas and weird sounds from the echoing caverns beneath, the terror was sufficient to turn one keeper's hair white in a single night and it is said that he went mad.

No place for a child you may be sure. But then Mary wasn't in the dark. Oh, but she was! The wind blew the (oil) light out and she was left with the task of relighting it. Easy for a man, but not for a child. She couldn't reach high enough. The only object available to stand on was a great Bible. For Mary it was sacrilege to stand on the Holy Book. In the end she decided, fearfully, that it would be better to run the risk of offending God in this way than to be responsible for leaving the shipping in the dark, so she stood on the Bible and lit the lamp. Read all about it in *The Watchers on the Longships* (J. F. Cobb, Wells Gardner, 1948 edition). The Bible has many uses.

Its main function, which we have left until last, is to equip men and women for fruitful and purposeful living; to reveal the ways of God to mankind; supremely to tell us the old, old story of Jesus who died on a cross. This is why in a rationalist and materialist age Christians may think nothing of using a copy of the Bible to prop up a projector. It's the message inside the book, not the paper that it's written on, that really matters. Some of us can't help feeling that it would be a better example to show some respect to the wrapper as well as the contents, but others will tell us that we are being superstitious and in danger of idolatry. Worshipping the Bible.

Why read the Bible?

Any discussion of the dangers of bibliolatry (using the Bible as an idol) is sure to lead to treading on somebody's toes, so, shoes and socks off, here we go.

Our problem is how to give the Bible the appropriate amount of respect as the word of God to us, without falling into the trap of making it central to our lives, usurping the throne that should be occupied by Jesus Christ himself. Some cynic once accused Bible-believing Christians of worshipping the Trinity of God the Father, God the Son and God the Holy Scriptures. How can we avoid falling into the opposite pitfalls of neglecting the words which can lead us to God and, as we noted on page 41, searching the Scriptures because we think we shall find life *in them* and failing to find Christ who is the true source of that life (John 5:£9–40)?

,4,10   First of all we need to settle on what we believe the Bible to be. Opinions vary, of course, but let me give you my working definition so that we know where we are. I believe that the contents of the Bible are there because God wanted them to be there. He put them into the minds of the writers and their editors so that what we now read is the most valuable book in the world. It gets us to the Truth behind all things. It shows us how to live and warns us how not to live. It is a basic handbook to equip God's people to live as he wants us to.

I have hinted at my suspicion that many more Bibles are sold than are actually read. Quite apart from propping up projectors and adorning wedding photographs there must be millions of copies in hotel bedrooms, on library shelves, provided as Sunday-school prizes and stockpiled so that each Christian household may 'boast' a dozen different versions. All this is very sad of course, but given the complexity of the Bible and the general lack of desire to know what is in it, not surprising.

What concerns me at this point is that many Bibles are being read but not acted upon. A gardening book will tell me how to grow flowers or improve my lawn. If I read it I may get a certain pleasure at second hand, but the purpose of the book is that I should get out there and *do* something in the garden. A novel has no such purpose. It is there to entertain. But the Bible is not there merely to entertain (although much of it is a very good read). It is there to show us how to live. If we read it and do not act upon it, it has failed in its purpose, or rather we have.

Jesus made precisely this point in his well-known

parable of the wise and foolish builders. The wise man built upon firm foundations and when the rains came his home stood firm. The foolish man built upon sand and great was the fall of his building. The point that is often missed is that the rock on which the first man built was not Christ or the church but the hearing and doing of Jesus' words. The man who merely heard and did not act on what he heard was the fool. More and more of us are beginning to feel uncomfortable. Why *do* we read the Bible? (I am addressing that rather small number of people who actually open the Bible for themselves, say at least once a week, regularly.)

If we get genuinely honest answers we should probably hear something like this: 'I read the Bible to get comfort. There are some lovely words in it. Psalm 23 is lovely.'

'I suppose I have to admit that I read the Bible out of habit. I was given a daily reading scheme as a child at Bible class and I've been doing it ever since. I find it helpful, of course, or I wouldn't do it, but, yes, basically out of habit.'

'Since we're all being honest I have to say that I read the Bible because the other members of my housegroup expect me to. I'd feel that I was letting them down if I didn't – well, all right, I'd be letting myself down in their eyes.'

'I read the Bible to learn about God and the world he created.'

'I read it for guidance. It tells me what to do when I'm stumped.'

'God speaks to me through his word. I can't hear his audible voice, but the Bible tells me what he wants me to know.'

'I read the Bible because it is the only book that reads me. It sets impossibly high standards, but it points me to Jesus who died to forgive my sin and failure and tells me about the Spirit of God who gives me some hope of living his way.'

I have no doubt that all of those answers are honest – the first three are creditable confessions. All are more or less positive and they get better as they go. But only the last one avoids the charge of using the Bible for our own convenience – reading it because it reads us (that can be extremely painful) and not for what we can get out of it, but   because God wants us to and it pleases him. In other words not duty, nor habit, nor profit, though all may be present, but basically through love, love for God who created us, Jesus who redeemed us and the Spirit who gives us new life.

Seeing what we expect to see

The most blatant form of bibliolatry is 'reading into' the Bible what we want it to say. I make up my own mind what is right about something and I pray about it (so that I can claim that God has shown me this particular truth) and then I 'prove' it by finding Bible verses that support what I want. Preachers sometimes fall into this trap. They listen to the buzzing of the fashionable bee in their bonnets, search the Scriptures, not for eternal life but for confirmation of their views, and hang their ideas on the biblical hooks they have found. Authors do it too . . . You must judge whether or not I am doing it now.

Let's take an example: a husband with chauvinist tendencies is at loggerheads with his wife who favours a feminist approach. Each will notice and approve the verses and chapters in the Bible which appear to support their case and ignore those which do not. Nothing surprising about this, but it goes deeper. The ignoring is not necessarily intentional nor even conscious. It's quite possible to intend to be open minded and still not even notice that something you didn't want to read was staring you in the face. There is a sort of switch in the mind which operates automatically to prevent our having to face unpalatable truth. (Conversely, of course, the pessimist, depressive or guilt-ridden person will always tend to stumble across passages and verses which they feared would be there – they are attracted to doom and gloom as a moth to its funeral pyre in a candle flame.)

But back to our opinionated couple. They read the passage in Ephesians (chapter 5, verses 22–33) where Paul describes the relationship of Christ and the church in terms of a marriage partnership. The husband reads as follows, 'Wives, be subject to your husbands as you are to the Lord. For the husband is the head of the wife just as Christ is the head of the church ... Husbands, love your wives ...' He points out that wives are called to be subject, husbands merely to love. Nothing could be clearer.

His wife, however, observes that he has stopped at a convenient place and omitted 'just as Christ loved the church and gave himself up for her'. The wife is called to be subject to her husband, but the husband is called to *sacrifice* himself for his wife, just as Christ did for the church. Which of these demands is the greater? And why had neither of them noticed the verse before the section began: 'Be subject to one another out of reverence for Christ.' So the wife is called to a submission which will make her 'radiant' (verse 27, NIV) and the husband to a lordship which will be utterly self-sacrificial. Two paradoxes; impossibly high standards, massive demands on the forbearance, love, trust and mutual support of both.

If our imaginary couple are really set in their prejudices, the calm discussion of such a passage will be beyond them. The fact that they have taken up positions on opposite sides will make it extremely difficult for either of them to admit to being wrong, even (or especially!) if they have a suspicion that they are. What hope is there then of the objective truth of the Bible, what God wants to say to us, getting through the thorny tangle of our preconceived ideas and prejudices? If it were not for the power of the Holy Spirit, breaking down such barriers, it might never happen, but we can co-operate with him and assist the process.

It is essential for us to come to the Bible in a spirit of prayerful readiness to learn. We need to be conscious that our minds are notoriously crooked and to be anxious to arrive at the truth of what we read, as far as possible untarnished by our own prejudice. Talking to God about it is always valuable. We are able to distance ourselves from our own narrow view of things if we discuss it with our creator. Talking to a friend or colleague can help us to be open to other views than our own too, and reading a good commentary (or, at best, more than one) can be an enormous help.

Interaction

Then come to the Bible text with as open a mind as possible and be ready to interact with it. By that I mean openly admit your own feelings about the passage concerned, but be ready for it to read you as well as your reading it. For instance look at the parable of the workers in the vineyard (Matthew 20:1–16). Many people have a hard job to understand this story, let alone agree with Jesus' teaching.

The landowner takes on labourers in the morning and they agree on a fair wage. As the day goes on more labourers are hired and all are promised a fair wage. At the last hour others are set on and have time to do very little work. When the wages are handed out these last receive a full day's wage. The others are at first delighted. They will surely receive more. But no, they all get the same. 'But this isn't fair! We've worked all day and get no more than these latecomers. We should have more.'

'Yes, I am being utterly fair,' says the landowner. 'I am honouring my agreement. You accepted the wage and I am now giving it to you. If I wish to favour others by gifting them in this way that is not your concern. I can give my money as I like.'

Now you may have to admit that your feelings are all on the side of the hard workers. Don't try to stifle those feelings because they are 'unsound' or because your minister tells you you're wrong. Bring your feelings of fair play and justice back to God and say to him, 'Look, I don't understand this. The landowner is being very unfair . . .' Even as I say this to God I almost hear him saying to me, 'You have the wrong word you know. He was not "unfair", but perhaps you think he was *unwise*. Perhaps he should have made his gifts to the latecomers in private and that would not have antagonized the others.'

So I come back to the passage, realizing that perhaps I have been feeling indignant for the wrong reason. And as soon as I look again I see the words 'The kingdom of heaven is like a landowner . . .' This is not a story about the vineyard really, it's a story about the kingdom of heaven. And it teaches that God is absolutely fair in that he gives his gracious love to everyone in equal measure, regardless of our shortcomings. It is not that some workers will be deprived of their rights but that all workers will be offered what they have not deserved anyway.

There may still be problems. The hard workers appear to have earned their way into the kingdom. Is that what Jesus intended? No. The whole point of the story is that the end result (entry to the kingdom of heaven) cannot be earned at all. It is a gift given equally to all who will receive it.

There is plenty of room for more interaction, but the point is we should be learning with the Scripture, discussing it with God, letting it inform our ideas and our feelings and re-reading it with new insights, retaining all the time our own judgment and feelings but getting ever nearer to the truth that is there.

The main feature of this approach is that we are interacting with the story, not either swallowing it whole or trying to deny it and we are spiralling in on the truth and relating more closely to God as we do so.

This kind of reading is not idolatry. In fact it is one of the strongest weapons we have against 'using' God to our own immediate advantages. We read the book: the book reads us. This is to our ultimate and eternal advantage, which is far better than anything short-term.

CHAPTER 10

Carrots and sticks

'Whose fault is it?' 'It's not *my* fault.' 'It's *your* fault.' Children in the playground. Yes, and let's admit it, grown-ups in their innermost thoughts. One of the most acute human faculties is our capacity for awarding blame. If anything goes wrong, our immediate reaction is to protest that it was not our fault (even if it was) and to try to discover who we should blame.

The washing-machine floods the kitchen floor. Wife: 'I told you this was going to happen one of these days.' Husband, sensing the meaning in the edge of her voice: 'Well, it isn't my fault! I don't supply washing-machines.' Wife, annoyed with both the washing-machine and her husband's defensiveness: 'I didn't say it was your fault, but somebody's to blame and somebody's got to take responsibility for it.'

'When was it last serviced?'

'About four years ago.'

'Well, perhaps it's your fault for not having it looked after properly.' There are seeds for a full-scale bust-up here and it would be painful to go on. Each tries to avoid blame and to find someone who is guilty.

At a more sombre level, have you noticed how the relatives and friends of a murder victim will sacrifice time and carefully amassed savings in order to find the murderer – sometimes for ten, twenty, thirty years? It can become almost an obsession. Some of these people are thirsty for vengeance, but I don't believe that they are all driven by the desire for retaliation. No, they need to know who was guilty. 'It's not knowing that is so hard.' It is difficult to explain, but it is an instinct deep down.

Real and home-made guilt

Perhaps the basic reason for our knee-jerk reactions to the matter of blame and guilt is that we are all in it up to our eyes. We *are* all guilty. Of something. We don't need the Bible to tell us about sin and that we all fall short of the glory of God. It is obvious to anyone who is honest enough to face up to the facts. Even if we manage to persuade ourselves that we have committed no specific crimes, sins or even misdemeanours (some of us are very persuasive when we are in dispute with our consciences), it is still not possible to claim that we have done everything that we *ought* to have done. The list is endless. We are by no means perfect and a great deal of mental and emotional anguish is caused by trying to justify ourselves and pretending that we are.

The familiar pattern is that we admit, of course, rationally and openly, that we are imperfect. Nobody's perfect. It would be arrogant of us to think we were. We confess our sins in church:

> Almighty God, our heavenly Father,
> we have sinned against you and against our fellow men,
> in thought and word and deed,
> through negligence, through weakness,
> through our own deliberate fault . . .
>
> (The Alternative Service Book, 1980)

Rationally and openly, with our thinking apparatus switched on, we accept that we are imperfect and need forgiveness. But emotionally, when our gut-feelings are consulted, we hear another tune being played. Our feelings tell us that we are innocent, or at least if we are guilty it isn't really our fault. It was our genes, our upbringing, our parents, that nasty accident, Satan, Adam and Eve, anyone's responsibility, but not mine. We are children, unwilling to take responsibility for our own faults, weakness and negligence. And of course the inner conflict between what we think and say we believe ('I am a sinner') and what we feel inside ('It's not my fault') causes all sorts of tensions, irritability, bad temper and sometimes clinical depression. Guilt, not properly faced, honestly admitted and genuinely forgiven can cause enormous damage to our peace of mind.

While one part of the world's population is trying to avoid confrontation with real guilt, another wide cross-section of society is wrestling with what I call home-made guilt. It isn't real guilt at all but imagined wrongs that I believe I have committed, failure to live up to proper standards (probably unwisely set by adoring parents who should have known better), seeing myself as inadequate and a failure.

Author Francis Schaeffer used to distinguish between these two kinds of guilt (the real and the home-made) as 'theological guilt' and 'moral guilt'. The good news is that real guilt, if it is faced and confessed, can be forgiven and removed by the mercy of God through the action of his Son Jesus Christ who sliced into our world 2,000 years ago to make this reconciliation possible. This is the core, the hub, of the Good News that Christianity has to offer. The bad news is that 'home-made guilt' cannot be forgiven. Why not? Is it so evil, that even the sacrifice of Christ on the cross will not demolish it? Not at all. The problem is that home-made guilt is imaginary. It does not really exist. You cannot be forgiven for a sin, failure or indiscretion that you have never committed.

It is very common for a bereaved person to feel guilt at the death of a loved one. We feel deeply that somehow, if only we had been better sons, daughters, brothers, sisters, that person might not have died. Our imagination roves to and fro, trying to find ways to blame ourselves. 'If only I had . . .' 'If only I hadn't . . .' Yet rationally it is very unlikely that you have been guilty of that person's death. You have spent your energies for weeks, months, even years, trying to keep him or her alive. Your guilt is not real. It is emerging from your overwrought imagination. You may need prayer, counselling, psychotherapy, or more likely time to get over it, but you do not need forgiveness for the death of your relative.

But there must be millions (I use that word carefully) of people who torment themselves day and night and plead to God for forgiveness for sins that they have never committed and ask his mercy for inadequacies which are totally imaginary and wonder why they feel no better but rather the worse.

So some people have sins which they can't face and so are never really forgiven, while others are confessing sins they have not committed (as well as the ones they have) and are in torment because they feel no forgiveness either. To add to those pernicious cocktails we might observe that most of us partake of both problems in some proportion so our capacity for self-deception and self-torture is almost infinite. If there were no personal power of evil, no devil of hell, we should need to invent him to explain our predicament. No wonder so many people turn to drink, drugs, crime or pure pleasure-seeking as a way out of the maze.

'My chains fell off'

We are following a very gloomy path from which there seems to be no exit. It is clear that drink, drugs and crime may deaden the pain of guilt for a time but, in the long term, do nothing but add to the sum of it. So what is the Christian way out? What did Christ achieve by entering our wicked world and ending up on the scaffold of a criminal? If that were the total picture he would have made things worse. But he did not 'end up' on the cross. There was an end after the end, a glorious postscript which saw him rise from death. In what we call the resurrection he called all his followers to rise with him, to say goodbye to the 'death' of unforgiven sins and the misery of self-reproach, and rise to a new life, guilt-free and light-hearted. Charles Wesley made the point with great clarity:

> Long my imprisoned spirit lay
>   Fast bound in sin and nature's night;
> Thine eye diffused a quickening ray, –
>   I woke, the dungeon flamed with light;
> My chains fell off, my heart was free,
> I rose, went forth, and followed Thee.

This is what is on offer and it's a thrilling prospect. Why is it then that so many *Christians* are still guilt-ridden? We have touched on one reason already. Some of us have been brought up to unreasonable expectations and a sense of failure has followed us through life. The mind-set of a lifetime does not always evaporate overnight. Also some Christian groups and churches seem almost obsessed with sin, its power and pervasiveness, and the struggles of the sinner to escape from its web result only in closer and more suffocating entanglement. Concentration on the disease rather than the cure, or better still the divine doctor, results in a deterioration of health. There may be other reasons too why Christians do not find that glorious peace of mind which some achieve. The point I want to make is this:

Forgiveness is probably mankind's greatest need. Without food we die. Without procreation the race dies. Without forgiveness we remain shut off from God and death becomes permanent. Humans need food, sex and forgiveness. And the greatest of the three is forgiveness. This may sound melodramatic but I believe it to be true. The essence of forgiveness is not feeling innocent again, feeling clean again or even feeling that chains have fallen off, though these are all on offer as it were as part of God's generosity. The essence of forgiveness is reconciliation, the restoration of relationship. This is so between people who have forgiven one another. It is equally so between ourselves and God. When we give in and show him the white flag and accept his forgiveness, there is peace between us and our relationship is restored, perhaps even established for the first time.

This forgiveness and reconciliation is open to all who will have it. It is dramatically expressed in Revelation chapter 3 where Jesus depicts himself as standing patiently outside the door of the individual's life and knocking for admittance. 'If you will open the door, I will come in and we shall eat together,' he says. Eating together is one of the best ways of expressing human friendship and fellowship. Jesus chooses this picture to explain how true forgiveness works. But notice that he says that we need to open the door, an act of the will; we do not necessarily need to feel elated. We hear his voice (realize what he wants) and respond. What happens is more important than what we feel. Some will feel immediate elation, others a quiet sense of warmth. But some may feel nothing at all, but need to rely on the promise made and the action taken. For such people the Lord's Supper, the Holy Communion, is very important, for here the eating with Christ and his people is physically demonstrated. If we cannot feel his forgiveness and his presence we can do better. We can obey his command: '*Do* this in remembrance of me.'

The divine carrot

So it is not necessary to *feel* the benefits of this wonderful reconciliation, but the fact remains that most people do and it is quite right that we should. To be reunited with the Father must have made the Prodigal Son's heart a great deal lighter and so it will do with most of us. God has implanted deep inside us all what some have called a 'God-shaped blank', a desire for communion with him. Just as the natural pangs of hunger are satisfied by a good meal, just as sexual desire is fulfilled when husband and wife make love together, so the need for reconciliation leads us on until we find that ultimate satisfaction in fellowship with our Maker, Defender, Redeemer and Friend.

So our detractors (and the perennially doubtful among the company of the faithful) can claim that we come to God merely to satisfy an inbuilt longing, a left-over primeval desire to merge with the ultimate, an urge to meet God. It turns out to be another form of idolatry after all; using God as a means to my own comfort and satisfaction. Preachers are accused of manufacturing a sense of guilt in their congregations so that they can 'sell' them the cure, the gospel.

What are we to say to these charges? When we feel low and dispirited we may believe them. And of course it may well be true. God does make eating pleasurable, otherwise, if it were a pain and a solemn duty, most of us would starve. And sex is a delight, otherwise the race would die out if the supreme expression of love was a matter of gloomy self-sacrifice. And so God has implanted in us a longing for himself. It is the divine carrot, if you like, that we human donkeys need to propel us into the kingdom of God.

Now the application of all this to the question of idolatry and the danger of using God is clear. We may not assume that because something is natural (like desiring God's love) it is therefore idolatrous. Just because something is pleasurable (like losing the chains of self-centredness and pride) does not make it wrong. There is a puritanical streak in many of us that promotes a feeling of guilt for enjoying anything. The Scottish minister who took a short cut over the ice and skated to church was accused of Sabbath-breaking on the grounds that he enjoyed the journey.

God 'richly provides us with everything for our enjoyment' (1 Timothy 6:17), and reconciliation with him is the richest cause for enjoyment imaginable. So whatever we do we must not fall into the trap of fearing that enjoyment is a form of idolatry. It *can* be, but it should not be. We must come back to this idea of enjoying God. It's too often neglected.

CHAPTER 11

Paying our way

Before we come to enjoying God, though, there's an extension to the problem of guilt which demands our attention. I mean trying to earn our salvation. Somebody has called it 'Pelagianism, the back door out of the gospel.'

Pelagius was a British Christian who lived in the fourth and fifth centuries. His teaching was that human nature is much stronger and morally better than orthodox Christians had allowed for. We are not *essentially* sinful. We need God's grace, to be sure, to save us, but it is basically up to us to perfect the goodness that is already there. His great emphasis, then, was on good works, good works which are achievable by the effort of our wills. This teaching plays straight into the hands of most of us because we naturally resent having to accept God's free forgiveness and feel that we must do something in return. In addition we are called frequently in the New Testament to good works – that was what we were created for (so said Paul in Ephesians 2:10). But it's all too easy to pay lip-service to salvation by grace and slip back into salvation by works.

Another temptation along the same lines is to 'salvation by service', feeling that by being someone important in the church's hierarchy we are being more acceptable to God.

The big fish and the busy trout

I notice two people in the shop and overhear their conversation:

'Good morning, John. I hope you're well.'

'Not too bad, thanks. How are you?'

'I've no time to be ill. I've got four meetings to go to today, *four*. And it's London again first thing in the morning. And again on Friday. It's all go, you know, all go. Goodbye.'

I know these people and I can't help wondering what they are thinking as they leave the shop. They are both retired and are both seen as 'pillars' of their churches, she of the Anglican, he of the Free Church.

She is thinking, 'Poor John. He really is a wimp. He's retired now and he has all the time in the world (I wish I had some of it) and yet he goes to that funny little chapel and he never seems to *do* anything – nothing for the community. He goes twice on Sundays and has at least two evening church meetings a week as far as I know, but that leaves four more evenings and I never see him at any of our political, social, fund-raising, tenants association, recreational or care-for-the-elderly meetings, to name but a few. He's totally immersed in his church and he's the most insignificant man I know. How grateful I am to be wanted and needed and fulfilled, even if I haven't time to think . . .'

He's thinking, 'Poor Mary. She really is a superficial workaholic. She rushes round like that I suppose because she's so insecure that she needs to feel that she's earning her place in society. It's not my business to judge her faith, or lack of it, but I can't see any evidence of it. All she does seems to be social work and because she keeps telling everyone how busy she is it makes us feel guilty because we aren't doing the same. But I know her family suffers. She's never at home.'

If that's what they are thinking about one another then neither is being charitable, but let's suppose we are able to see them both as they really are. What might we find?

John certainly has faith. He became a firm Christian believer as a teenager and has never wavered into serious doubt. He has worshipped at the same church for all his life, working locally and never living more than a few miles away. Naturally he has become a respected member of the fellowship. He has held various offices. In fact within the confines of his church he is A Very Significant Person. When you go to a service, there you will find him standing by the door looking Important. When the offering is taken up, he it is who takes it. When the notices are given out, he it is who gives them. John is a very large fish. His whole world is the goldfish bowl of the chapel. In it he Matters. He is Somebody. He rarely, if ever, thinks how small is the bowl and what a tiny world he bestrides. John is right in not finding his significance in workaholism, but he has surrendered to another temptation: self-importance.

Mary, on the other hand, has no time to consider her own importance. She is too busy, responding to every real (and imagined) call on her time. She too has a real faith, but it has become gradually buried beneath the debris of all her good works. Her church does not help. The Vicar lets it be known that much needs to be done, that faith is best expressed in good works (and who can deny that?). It is also clear, and here is a parallel with John's situation, that the Top People in the church are those who Do Most. Those who are not overworking are looked down on by the others. She is not led but driven, driven by her own mistaken perfectionism, which is fuelled by the church's emphasis on practical commitment. Mary is right not to find her significance in self-importance. She is, after all, a work-aholic.

True significance

Let it not be thought that the best Christians are those who are insignificant, hold no office and do no good works. We all need to be significant, to know that we matter, and there is work for everyone. Perhaps we shall get the right perspective if we imagine John and Mary being interviewed by Peter, the doorkeeper of heaven. An angel hands him papers:

Peter: 'I see that both of you have permits of entry. That is good and you are welcome. Before you go in, however, I have a few questions to ask. Mary first. On what grounds do you claim to come in?'

Mary: 'Well, I have burned myself out in the Master's service. I have averaged two and a half meetings a day for the past twenty-five years, sat on seventeen committees, travelled over a million miles . . .'

Peter (quietly): 'And worn out your husband?'

Mary: 'My husband has been very supportive. I have anyway done all those things,' she finishes lamely.

Peter (even more quietly): 'But, Mary, who told you to do all those things? Was it God? I think not. You *are* accepted here, not because of what you have done but because of who you are. The Master loved you so much that his Son died for you. That is your value. You are welcome. Now John, what say you?'

John: 'I have done nothing worth mentioning. I cannot claim to have qualified myself by good works. I am a humble servant, chairman, treasurer, steward, deacon, elder and secretary in the Lord's service.'

Peter: 'Thank you, John. Yes, you are accepted here, but not because of who you are but because of what Christ has done. Medals are not worn here, you know. There is an exceedingly great reward awaiting you, but you will have to resign from all your positions of office first. Then, you are welcome too.'

The success factor

A third thumbnail sketch comes in the form of part of a letter from Jim and Alison. They are part-time workers with a well-known Christian organization and are committed to raising some of their own support. They send out regular 'prayer letters' to their support group, the people who donate to their work. Here is an extract from one of them:

> The Lord is greatly blessing our work in which you share. In recent weeks we have seen many lives touched by him. Our meetings have been well attended and we've sold good numbers of booklets.
>
> Our plans are taking shape for next year. We are doubling the number of centres from which we operate and we need more helpers in these areas. We feel that the Lord is moving mightily and that great things are about to happen. Thank you for your part with us in this wonderful work.

In reality Jim and Alison are good-hearted, enthusiastic Christians who have felt a genuine call to their work. After doing it for two and a half years, however, they are beginning to question how valuable it is and whether they have really made very much progress. They are getting rather despondent about their lack of 'success'. This, of course, they dare not communicate to their supporters, partly because it is always hard to admit that you are not doing great things for the Lord, much harder still to explain that, as far as you can see, the Lord is not doing great things for you, as the book says that he always will; and anyway they might withdraw their financial as well as prayer support. It becomes necessary to unpack the message of their letter and look at the hidden meaning.

'The Lord is greatly blessing our work.' At worst this means that it's the kind of opening a warm supporter wants to hear. It's the jargon. At best it means that, although there are many discouragements, we believe that God is always with us and has not deserted us.

'We have seen many lives touched by him.' The unwritten meaning here is, 'We hope that people have been helped by what we have done, but we cannot quote any concrete evidence for it. We have spoken to people and they have listened and we trust that God will use all this to his glory.' At worst this is another jargon-phrase that will make the supporters feel good.

'Our meetings have been well attended and we've sold good numbers of booklets.' If the meetings had been really well attended actual numbers would have been quoted. Hundreds, even fifties, sound encouraging. The truth is, 'Attendance at our meetings has averaged seventeen, and over the past year we have sold seventy-one booklets. As they are very cheap, however, we are not really confident that anyone has *read* them. They probably buy them out of politeness.'

'We are doubling the number of centres from which we operate.' Talk of plans for the future sounds positive and inspiring. Doubling the number of centres feels like an ambitious step of faith. In fact there are at present three centres functioning and the proposed increase in a year is a further three. As it happens this is unrealistic because Jim and Alison are already working full-time at what is supposed to be a part-time job. They do not have the energy to sustain any more growth but will not admit it, even to themselves. More helpers are certainly needed. Realistically most people who could help have already got too much to do, but to be fair, it may be that the Lord has some people who could take on the task. Now comes the climax.

'We feel that the Lord is moving mightily and great things are about to happen.' How often, in say the past ten years, have you heard it said that somebody, some important Christian-body *feels* that the Lord is moving mightily ... this year ... or next spring ... or in the region of Manchester or Cincinnati? And how often have you checked up the following year or spring, or in the environs of Manchester, to see in what mighty way God has moved in response to their feeling?

Please don't misunderstand me. These questions may sound cynical, but they are not. I fully believe that God can and does move mightily but that very often his movements cannot be measured or even noticed by his people. I am trying to be honest and to ask what sort of weight we should attach to this kind of talk. If God doesn't obviously 'move' in Manchester and the original speaker is challenged about it there is a danger in his/her making up some justification for it, after all something good must have happened recently in Manchester. (Mancunians, please forgive me. I have chosen the name at random and am not conducting a campaign against you.)

Moreover, even if God is about to do something extraordinary next year in the lives of Jim and Alison, I don't think we should expect him to have to alter their feelings today. It can happen and it sometimes does (although it's fatally easy to 'remember' the feeling that something would happen after it has), but I wonder whether it happens as often as we are led to believe. This sounds very much like another hopeful jargon-phrase to please the readers.

We may well castigate the 'prosperity gospel', the idea that God will give success to all the faithful. But are we not all in danger of 'paying our way' by either going flat out for 'success' in the Lord's service (how *do* you measure it anyway?) or encouraging the idea in others by praising the 'successful' and blaming the merely faithful who show no 'results'? And if we can point to no success where we are, we salve our consciences by praying for and giving aid to those more unfortunate than ourselves – the 'Third World'.

Prayer and giving aid are just the things God wants us to indulge in, but from what motive? To please him, or as a signal to others and ourselves that we are being model, successful Christians? It's a narrow line of demarcation.

Keeping the idols happy

Mary, John, Jim and Alison are all trying to justify themselves, to prove to themselves, to other people and to God that they are worthy, that they deserve goodwill and reward for their behaviour. Put like that it sounds terribly childish, and in fact it is. We all have a strong temptation to be like this because we have not become adult in our attitudes. We know that we cannot earn our salvation and that it is all given to us by the grace of God *and yet* we still revert to Pelagianism, the back door out of the gospel.

It is ironical that Jesus put it the other way round: not 'Children, you must become adult to enter the kingdom. You will understand later when you're old enough,' but 'Adults you must become as little children or you will never see the kingdom of God.' A really small child may be totally dependent on adults and exhibits that childlike trust that does not try, does not need, to justify itself. That is what Christ hopes to find in us.

How far have we strayed from the subject of idolatry? Not a whisker. The committed idol-worshipper has two major concerns: one is to procure safety, comfort, fertility or whatever seems desirable;

the other is to avoid upsetting the idol by bringing the wrong offerings, reciting the wrong prayers or behaving badly. In other words idols need to be propitiated, kept friendly by our good behaviour. If we behave badly, or are unsuccessful, then the idol will punish us by refusing to grant what we want.

If we approach God in this way, trying to keep him on our side by good behaviour or catalogues of good works, we are using him as an idol. The truth, the life-giving, refreshing truth is that all the propitiating has been done and we are free to come to God as our Father. We are his adopted children and we do not have to justify ourselves to him. Just say thank you for his love.

CHAPTER 12

United we evaluate

I s it worth it?
   This is a perfectly proper question and one which
is frequently asked. That suit will cost £75; this dress
will be $200. Are they worth it? If we don't possess that
kind of money the question is purely academic; it
doesn't affect us personally. But suppose we are fortunate enough to have the means to buy the suit or the
dress, what do we imply?

Is this garment important enough to me at the
moment to warrant my spending the money on it?
Have I enough suits or dresses so that getting another
one would be pure greed or vanity or do I really need
it? If I need it (and that means that, compared with
other needs, it comes out near the top), can I be sure
that it's the colour I want? the right material? the
appropriate cut? Will it wear well? Will it be easy to
clean? How will it compare in price with other items of
clothing that I have bought and other people have told
me about?

I decide to go to the theatre. The tickets seem expen-
sive. The cheapest ones, I know, procure seats on back-
less benches, stacked up in the roof, looking down
almost vertically on to a distant stage with no hope of
hearing anything. So how do I decide whether it's
'worth' paying say £15.00 for a better seat? Is the play
well-known? entertaining? stirring? improving? or is it
likely to be depressing or degrading? Have I been a lot

to the theatre recently or is this a rare treat? What occasion, if any, am I celebrating? Who am I going with (congenial company may make the subject matter of the play less important!).

All of this is so familiar and commonplace that we do it without analysing it as I have done and you may be getting impatient with all this all-too-obvious business. What's the point?

Healing and teaching for profit

The point that I want to make is that this 'Is it worth it?' approach is so familiar and so deeply ingrained in us that we are liable to use it on everything, whether it's appropriate or not. Current political thinking, in the West at least, tends to reduce all the joys as well as necessities of life to questions of commercial interest, market values and what things are 'worth'. Even fifty years ago it was possible to believe the popular song, 'The best things in life are free.' The 1990s remind us that 'There's no such thing as a free lunch.' The health service and education as well as building works, road-making and manufacture are evaluated from the standpoint of how much they will cost and what will be the financial profit from the success of the operation.

Do you know how many million pounds worth of person-hours are lost every year through back-trouble? I can't remember either. The figures are sometimes advertised so that industry, aware of this potential financial saving, will be careful of its workers and try to prevent their absence. Never mind their suffering of course. Just think of it in terms of lost revenue.

Educationists today do not seem to argue, as they did in the 1950s, about what is the meaning of an excellent life towards which we are leading our children. To develop the imagination, to improve their innate gifts, to help them to be better people in society; those were some of the ideas we discussed. But today we are being challenged to ask 'Is that worth it?' How much will young Kevin earn as a result of his education? That's what we ought to be asking. It is perhaps ironical that in the fifties when we debated the meaning of life and the pursuit of excellence there was plenty of employment available. Now we are 'educating' people to make a material impact and earn a high wage, they are much more likely to remain unemployed.

I am in danger of digressing, but I have at least stated my own view (call it prejudice if you like) that healing and education are two areas in which the end result ought not to be calculated in sterling or Deutsche Marks. Neither should hospitals or schools be run as profit-making industries. I do not mean that they should not be run in a business-like way: well-organized, reducing waste to a minimum, efficient and purposeful. But it will never be cost-effective to educate a severely handicapped child, or to provide a full range of care for the elderly and fragile. To see education and health care in terms of cash and profitability will soon lead to the marginalization (dreadful word) of those people, treating them not as people at all but as products of the system and products which will soon be seen as unwanted refuse.

Is the church worth it?

Now, how am I to assess the value of a church? What makes it 'worth it'? We have already overheard the little lady who greatly appreciated the availability of her 'little church' and said how much better she felt for the 'little services'. We suggested that she was at least being positive and that some good was coming out of her attendance. She felt better. She was, of course, expressing in her own words the idea that it was worth it to go to that church. The effort of getting out and sacrificing a couple of hours by the fire, the cost of putting her collection on the plate, were 'worth it' for the benefits she received. Again, let's not be hard on this lady. If people look at church attendance in the light of profit and loss and see it as profit, rejoice and be glad! There are many who see it as loss and have given it all up.

On the other hand, this approach has its negative aspect. Have you ever heard this kind of conversation after a service? Gerry meets Nick, over coffee.

'What did you think of him (meaning the preacher) this morning then?'

'I found it very helpful, what he said. Very enlightening. What did you think?'

'He did nothing for me.'

'I'm sorry to hear that. I thought he was lively with plenty of up-to-date relevance, as they say.'

'Yes, I suppose so.'

'And biblical.'

'Oh, yes, he's biblical.'

'And a good balance of warm encouragement and challenge to think matters through and act on our principles. All this sounds like a preacher's handbook. What is your problem with him?'

'It's like I said, he does nothing for me. I come here on a Sunday after a week of pressure one way or another, at work, at home with the kids, no time for spiritual things, if you know what I mean. So I come here drained and waiting to be filled. And I sit there through the sermon and I don't feel any better at the end of it. Just the same in fact.'

Gerry is about to say something in reply to this when they are joined by their wives. So he addresses Nick's wife instead.

'Sue, what do you think? Nick says that Bob (the

minister) does nothing for him. He feels just as bad now as he did when he came in.'

'Well, Nick and I have a different approach to Bob. I really find him quite helpful. I don't want to disagree with you in public, Nick, but a couple of things he said this morning really rang bells with me. He said the same things that I'd read in my Bible-reading notes. Either God is nudging me or it's a very odd coincidence.'

'It's all very well,' says Nick, 'for people who have time to read the Bible, and we don't have to agree about everything, but what about worship, Sue?'

'Oh dear, that's where we *do* agree. It's pitiful isn't it? I mean all those boring old hymns . . .'

'We had a session of choruses today and the rest were all from *Mission Praise*.'

'There you are! Condemned out of your own mouth. *Mission Praise* is years out of date. Nobody who knows anything sings them any more. And one of the choruses we sang this morning came from CSSM choruses, about 80 years old!' (Nick and Sue laugh loudly.) 'At the Sharpfield Community church they've just gone on to *Rend the Heavens* Book 2. That's really up to date. The worship there really does things for me.'

'So,' says Nick, rather hesitantly, 'that's why we're thinking of moving over to Sharpfield. The preaching meets my needs and the worship meets Sue's.'

'And the fellowship there is really great,' says Sue, warming to her subject, now the difficult admission has been made. 'You're *really* welcome there. They'd do anything for you. There's a lovely warm and caring atmosphere. We're going to be really happy there, I know it, I can *feel* it.' They wave goodbye, leaving Gerry and his wife temporarily speechless and feeling about two inches high. Gerry breaks the silence,

'I wonder how long they'll last there?'

'Six months would be a record. May we be forgiven for being cynical.'

Past experience suggests that she is not being cynical but realistic. Nick and Sue regard a church as a place and a community, tailormade to suit their needs. If it fails to reach their standards, does not produce the right feelings, then they must change it for another one. Another suit, another dress, another seat at the theatre, another form of education, another doctor, if this one doesn't cure me instantly . . .

The two-way process

There can be no doubt that some churches are very unhelpful, churches where the Bible is not respected, where even Christ is not honoured, where members are not cared for, the poor not prayed for and where the whole organization seems to proceed independently of God altogether. 'The Second Coming will take place on Sunday afternoon,' announces the angel. 'Evening service as usual at 6.30 pm, DV', says the notice.

Live Christians are needed in dead churches so that they can bring the churches back to life, but not all are called to this very tough, front-line ministry. Most of us are fragile and like Nick we need to be fed and nourished spiritually: we need the support of the fellowship and real life in Christ. After prayer and heart-searching it may be necessary for us to leave that dying church because it is clearly taking us down with it. It may be failing our children.

But most churches are not like that. The 'pick 'n' mix', 'choose-what-suits-me' attitude of the day means that hundreds of people are deserting churches that are quite capable of supporting them and nourishing them too if they could but see the need for a two-way process; not just, 'What can I get out of this church?' but also, 'What can I put into it?'

That sermon may have 'done' nothing for you, but did you do anything for the preacher? Pray for him? Listen carefully to what he was saying? Prepare yourself to act on his suggestions? The worship may not have made you feel better but what do the other members of the church feel about it? What about God? Is he pleased only when you 'feel' better? And how many people change churches because they can't 'get on' with the new minister, the new vicar, the elders, a female incumbent?

This last problem cannot be discussed here but it raises the question of principle. There may well be matters of deeply-felt and long-thought-out conviction which mean that we cannot, in good conscience, continue with the present leader. For some people women's ordination will be one of those convictions. Other matters of conscience might involve homosexuality, immoral behaviour or heretical beliefs, any of which aspects of a pastor's life will make some unable to continue to support them. These people should not be encouraged to swallow their scruples and stay where they cannot find fellowship with the minister whom they see as at fault.

Having said all this, however, and allowing for exceptions and hard cases, it is the idolatry factor that urges us to get what we can out of churches and give nothing back; to demand what suits me. Oh yes, it is quite possible for the church leadership to be biblical, organized and caring and still lack that vital spark of Christian love, the glowing presence of the Holy Spirit. But if you leave for that reason, one more channel of that love and that spirit will be lost. Please leave only if you really must.

Incidentally it is curious that we have dubbed as

idolatrous two approaches to the church which appear to be total opposites. John and Mary, in chapter eleven, were at fault because they were trying to do too much for their churches, while Nick and Sue have failed because they are interested only in what they can get out of the many churches they have joined. Surely they're not all wrong? But yes. These two examples show us the opposite faces of idolatry: the aspect of fear and desire to please, and the aspect of using the idol to obtain our own desires. One can well imagine what it is like when these two are both present in the same person, as they often are!

Last word to the minister

Whenever anyone leaves a church because it is distasteful to him it is the minister who suffers most. It's a vote of no confidence in him or her. Even if the move was not intended to involve personalities, the pastor will feel it personally.

You talked to them, prayed for them, prayed with them, visited them, did all you could and still they left. You feel bruised, dispirited and discouraged. Perhaps the only comfort, if comfort it be, is to remember that our Lord went that way too. Not just a trickle of followers left (after those 'hard sayings' about eating his flesh and drinking his blood for instance, many deserted him), but when the real test came, all his *disciples* even, forsook him and fled. Be comforted then. Your case is not as bad as his and he understands.

There is a danger that you will accuse yourself of failure. That Nick and Sue's leaving is your fault. You can't forgive yourself. But Jesus can forgive you and nine times out of ten it isn't your fault anyway.

Occasionally, however, it might be. Are you sure that you are not being a bit too authoritarian? Are you really shepherding your flock or marshalling it? Most ministers are humble folk who listen to criticism and act upon it, who see themselves as facilitators, privileged to assist the Lord in his work of mending broken people. But there are a few who are naturally inclined to be martinets, who see their calling from God as an absolute demand to get their will done in their own way. And label it as God's will and way.

If you are one of those people you will probably not understand the last paragraph or at least you will believe that it applies to others, not to yourself. But please just consider that it might be you. The idolatry of the priesthood/pastorship/ministry is perhaps the most dangerous idolatry of all, when your people become less important to you than the system you believe to be correct, and love becomes subservient to the doctrines that you believe to be vital. As Oliver Cromwell wrote to the General Assembly of the Church of Scotland in 1650, 'I beseech you, in the bowels of Christ, think it possible you may be mistaken.'

CHAPTER 13

Happiness

It is time to return to what could be the most power-ful idol of them all: happiness. Christians are notor-iously double-minded about happiness. We feel uncomfortable about wanting to be happy and yet our deepest desires demand happiness for ourselves. But why do we feel uncomfortable about it?

I think there are two reasons. The first we might label theological. A Christian is a person who has renounced sin and selfishness. 'Take my life, and let it be ... ever, only, all for Thee', wrote Frances Ridley Havergal. What concerns us now is the glory of God and the well-being of our fellow humans. Our own feelings should come last. A life of pleasure-seeking is the life of the world and we renounce it. The world believes that it has a *right* to pursue happiness; we believe that happiness is a gift which we may be for-tunate to receive but it should not be sought.

Some Christians prefer to distinguish between happiness and joy. Happiness is equated with pleasure and its pursuit, hedonism. Joy is defined as well-being in Christ, a deep-seated knowledge that all is well and will ever be well, even if we *feel* unhappy. Christ promised his followers suffering as well as peace and joy, so we cannot claim a feeling of happiness to be part of God's purpose for us.

A second reason for some people's guilt about happiness is the unfairness of it all. Thousands destroy one another in war, millions are starving and literally thousands of millions are deeply unhappy. It seems that the common lot of humanity is to be unhappy. That is why so many frantically search for happiness, to escape from the normal gloom which pervades our society. So what right have I to be happy when so many are miserable? And if I am happy, should I not feel guilty in the face of the injustice? So say many.

Confusing the issue still further is the fact that some are temperamentally sunny and optimistic and are quite likely to be happy compared with others who, whatever their circumstances, tend to be glum and to see the worst in everything.

The fact remains that most people with no religion spend their lives looking for happiness, not super-thrills, sixty a minute, but a general feeling of well-being, spiced with fun and excitement when required. Whether anybody ever reaches that plane for more than a short time is open to question. What we are concerned about here is the Christian's approach.

There are a few mortals who renounce happiness as a snare of the devil and seem actively to seek unhappiness. They have seen through the tinsel of the world's glitter and fear its temptations. Those are the ascetics who deny pleasure and embrace pain for the Lord's sake. A generous assessment suggests that these people receive a deep-down joy in exchange for their denial of pleasure. The cynic responds, 'There you are: it's their pleasure to deny themselves so they're no less pleasure-seeking than the rest of us. They just look for it in odd places.'

But most of us are inconsistent, confused and ambivalent towards happiness – we desire it very strongly. We see the danger in pleasure-seeking, the danger that we might be too worldly, embracing the search for happiness as our idol. So we repent of our idolatry and find happiness in worship and fellowship. We feel guilty for being happy in this way, but devastated when we're unhappy. Where are we going wrong? An example might help.

Happy Christmas?

I am writing this chapter as Christmas approaches. Annual letters and greetings cards are already flying round the world in blizzards as we all pause to wish one another a happy Christmas. On 25th December, 'Good morning' or 'Hi!' or whatever greeting we normally use, gives way to 'Happy Christmas!' But what exactly do we mean by those two words? There are probably as many meanings as there are people who say the greeting, but we might summarize them at four distinct levels.

Level one is the obvious meaning, and probably the one most usually intended. 'Happy Christmas' means, 'Have for yourself a pleasurable time. Be warm and comfortable, enjoy plenty to eat and drink and receive the presents you hope for.' This is the level of pure self-centred hedonism and is what we have already been discussing. Happiness of this kind is not wrong in itself and it is a pity if Christians live down to their negative reputation as kill-joys and Scrooges. But if 'Happy Christmas' is an onion then this meaning is the outer skin of the onion and is very superficial.

The second layer of 'happiness' extends beyond the individual to the family and our friends. For many, Christmas is still the family time when relations do their best to visit one another, children are indulged and given treats, friends drop in for a mince pie and we derive pleasure from giving hospitality and presents as well as receiving them. This layer is not purely selfish. It is not only a search for pleasure (though it is in part), at least not merely *my* pleasure. It is shared pleasure and is much richer and more satisfying than the selfish kind. And consequently the happiness is deeper and more enduring. All of this is common sense.

What other layers are there to enjoying Christmas? The third layer I call 'Back to our roots.' I realize that much of the tradition of Christmas derives from Northern Europe and most of it from the nineteenth century. So we behold the spectacle of secular or Shinto-centred Japan lit up with Santa Claus and red-nosed reindeer in lights, and sweltering Australians singing 'In the bleak mid-winter' in midsummer. So what I am about to say will have a European bias and needs to be translated.

Whatever form it takes, the happiness of Christmas is greatly enhanced by the realization that we are linked with the past by a long succession of Christ-masses receding into the dim and ancient past. Father Christmas, Christmas cards and Christmas trees, robins (the 19th-century postmen in England wore scarlet uniforms and were known as 'robins'), stage-coaches and bow-fronted shops are all characteristics of the Victorian Christmas. The English Victorians were gluttons for sentimentality as well as good food if they could get it, and all these apparently essential trappings of Christmas became fixed in our hearts as 'Christmassy'. More recently still the 20th century has provided us with teddy bears and the Festival of Nine Lessons and Carols, which owes its popularity to radio.

But go back further. Feasting at Yuletide, the mid-winter festival, has a very long ancestry, certainly pre-Christian. Turkey and plum pudding are relatively recent acquisitions (the former of course from the States), while mince pies used to be made of minced meat and fruit, and beef has long been eaten at Christmas. Decorations of holly and ivy and other evergreens, no doubt presaging the undying greenness of nature and the coming of the new year, and mistletoe with its symbolism of fertility, the burning of the Yule log, all these take us back into the dark ages and long before. What ancient half-memories of our ancestry are not aroused by 'the holly and the ivy', 'the rising of the sun and the running of the deer' and the medieval pious addition of the 'playing of the merry organ [*i.e.* pipes], sweet singing in the choir'?

Many of the old carols (formerly *dances*) that have come down to us carry a heady mixture of medieval folk-beliefs and Christian doctrine. Who can fail to be stirred at this time of year by a deep happiness that springs from our getting in touch, however briefly and superficially, with our own distant past, and experiencing once more the moving of we know not what deeply hidden emotions. We are one with our heritage, and just once a year we step aside from the computerized world of air travel, TV channels, hypermarkets and plastics to 'hear again the message of the angels'.

Now I have already strayed beyond the third layer – which is largely fuelled by folk-memory and consciousness of human continuity – into the fourth and deepest source of happiness, the story of the Christ-child. It is hard for us to bridge the gap of two thousand years, to appreciate the reality of the Christmas story. Some of us can't believe it anyway; it sounds too much like a fairy story, and its constant repetition every year reinforces that feeling. But even those of us who do believe that it all happened even as the Bible says it did, have difficulty in *realizing* the story, feeling it as real as well as merely acknowledging it.

For me the third layer of my onion, the long-distance succession of Christmasses, helps to make the connection. That long succession does not stretch into a past infinity, like a hall of mirrors. It comes to an abrupt stop at the manger in a cattle shed or cave in Bethlehem. And, after all, it's only eighty generations. If a centenarian could tell the good news of Christ's coming to a little child and that message be passed by word of mouth, it would have needed only twenty people to link the first century with ours!

If we can grasp that the Nativity is relatively recent and utterly real we are in a good position to receive the happiness that flows inevitably from the Good News. The message of the angels was the best news mankind could ever hope for. 'Glory to God in the highest' (turn away from ourselves and greet our Creator as he should be greeted) 'and on earth peace to men' (the war between God and mankind is now over; may we follow God's example and pursue peace among ourselves) 'on whom his favour rests' (God's *favour* rests on *us*! What could make us happier than that?).

So a really happy Christmas, at the deepest level, involves our reaching out across the centuries to receive that declaration of God's favour, and as we reach out to touch, as it were, the manger, we discover that his favour is around us and within us already. The gulf has been bridged. 'Blessed ['happy' or 'fortunate'] are those who hunger and thirst for righteousness, for they will be filled' (Matthew 5:6).

That kind of happiness is not limited to the Christmas season. It is possible at any time and must surely not be refused. It is OK to be happy! If we find our happiness as the result of a search for God then we are happy indeed. If we pursue happiness as an end in itself we use God as a means to happiness, we turn him into an idol and deep unhappiness is the result. Once again it is a question of motives and attitudes. 'Take delight in the LORD, and he will give you the desires of your heart' (Psalm 37:4).

'Christian hedonism'

In his book *Desiring God*, John Piper has introduced many readers to the idea of 'Christian hedonism'. This phrase gives most of us a nasty jolt because the words seem to contradict one another. Hedonism is the word used for the pursuit of pleasure, not just as an every-day experience but as a philosophy of life, the very idolatry that we have been warned against. How can this be Christian? 'Why,' answers Piper, 'by enjoying God.' You can neither love, nor enjoy, an idol. It provokes fear. We must come back to this. But if we really love God we shall enjoy him.

The seventeenth-century Westminster Confession declared that our chief end (aim in life) is to glorify God and enjoy him for ever. Piper suggests that we could amend that slightly without damage to the sense and read, 'The chief end of man is to glorify God *by enjoying* him for ever.'

If you want the whole argument (which is based entirely on Scripture by the way) then read the book, but an outline may help. A powerful element in Piper's 'conversion' to Christian hedonism was reading a ser-mon by C. S. Lewis entitled 'The weight of glory'. Part of it goes like this:

> If there lurks in most modern minds the notion that to desire our own good and earnestly to hope for the enjoyment of it is a bad thing, I submit that this notion has crept in from Kant and the Stoics and is no part of the Christian faith. Indeed, if we consider the unblushing promises of reward and the staggering nature of the rewards promised in the Gospels, it would seem that our Lord finds our desires not too strong, but too weak. We are half-hearted creatures, fooling about with drink and sex

and ambition when infinite joy is offered us, like an ignorant child who wants to go on making mud pies in a slum because he cannot imagine what is meant by the offer of a holiday at the sea. We are far too easily pleased.

(C. S. Lewis, *The Weight of Glory and other Addresses*, quoted in J. Piper, *Desiring God* [Multnomah Press, 1986; IVP, 1989], pp. 15–16)

We were created with an appetite for happiness, which God entirely approves as it is meant to lead us to him. But we have preferred to look for happiness in the wrong places and have missed it altogether. And missed God into the bargain.

Piper clarifies this as follows:

Christian Hedonism is a philosophy of life built on the following five convictions:

1. The longing to be happy is a universal human experience, and it is good, not sinful.

2. We should never try to deny or resist our longing to be happy, as though it were a bad impulse. Instead we should seek to intensify this longing and nourish it with whatever will provide the deepest and most enduring satisfaction.

3. The deepest and most enduring happiness is found only in God.

4. The happiness we find in God reaches its consummation when it is shared with others in the manifold ways of love.

5. To the extent we try to abandon the pursuit of our own pleasure, we fail to honor God and love people. Or, to put it positively: the pursuit of pleasure is a necessary part of all worship and virtue. That is,

The chief end of man is to glorify God
BY
enjoying him for ever.

(J. Piper, p. 19)

On this view, what many Christians have thought of as a dangerous idol turns out to be nothing less than the way to God himself. How important it is to distinguish between what is true worship and what is idolatrous. This we must now do.

CHAPTER 14

Hard-core reality

In the course of the past thirteen chapters we have picked up and examined a number of the pebbles of the Christian's life, and put them down again. Prayer, protection, peace of mind, healing, worship, guidance, Bible-reading, forgiveness, service, fellowship, happiness . . . There are probably more areas that should be looked at, but we have only two chapters remaining and we need to address the two vital questions: What is at the root of all these problems? and, Is there any solution to them?

Earlier we discovered that there is no easy division of activities between idolatrous and true. To pray for a parking place may be an example of trying to make use of God for our own convenience, but it could be the helpless plea of a needy driver, calling on the only source of help available. The idolatry factor depends on circumstances and our attitude.

Does this mean then that, whenever I have a decision to make, I must do an analysis of my motives, my feelings, my attitude, to discover whether I am facing the right way? If I do this, will I not end up more confused than before?

Certainly it can be very beneficial, when taking big steps in life, like assessing a new job, or whether to propose (or accept an offer of marriage) to stand back and question our inner drives, to ask whether we are purely selfish or genuinely desirous of doing what is right. But imagine doing an in-depth analysis of one's attitude when deciding what to cook for lunch . . .

'Dad, why is Mum sitting at the kitchen table with a tea-towel over her head? Is she ill?'

'No, son, she's analysing her attitude and trying to decide whether it would be idolatrous to cook what she likes best today, which is fish, or what I like best, which is chops.'

'She's *what*?'

'Like I said, she's . . .'

'But Dad, *I* like baked beans. And I'm hungry.'

No, many of our daily decisions, relationships and actions are governed by our deep-down attitudes without our needing to dig them up and examine them. We are on auto-pilot. We follow our natural instinct for what is right without rational debate. We do, in other words, what we are. A person naturally cheerful will spread warmth and comfort; a naturally gloomy person will infect us with greyness. An outward-going personality will be likely to 'go for it' and make the bold decision; a timid and sensitive person will be likely to hesitate and to compromise.

What price 'natural instincts'?

We are edging nearer to the core of the matter. We are governed, in part, by our personality, the kind of person we happen to be. Is that all? By no means. We are also strongly influenced by our upbringing and environment (which have a lot to answer for in forming our personality) and also by our world-view, the way our mind and our feelings see things.

It is my contention that the 'natural' world-view of the vast majority of the inhabitants of this planet (if not all of us) tends towards idolatry. Deep down that is what we are like.

In case there are still some lingering doubts about

what I mean, may I repeat that I do not mean that most people possess carved images which they worship, nor do I mean that most people have a material god which they put first in their lives, though this is obviously true in a world of money, comfortable houses, motor-cars, fashionable clothes and so on.

No, what I mean is that we naturally tend to need a Something or Someone to which (or whom) we can look as the source of help for us and which (or who) needs to be kept friendly towards us by our good behaviour or sacrifices. People whom the West condescendingly calls 'developing' may openly come to their idols in such hope and fear. The superior Westerners may invest just as much energy of hope and fear in superstition which scorns graven images but craves for astrological signs and worships at the shrine of 'luck'. The surface, rational, common-sense approach to life is at war with the feelings, the gut-reaction which responds with fear and a desire to manipulate events through the occult or superstition.

Now in theory Christians have turned their backs on all this. The 'god-shaped blank' has been filled by the presence of Christ, the Spirit of the Living God. We are no longer at the mercy of deep-down fears of 'what might be' and we do not need to manipulate the hidden forces because we are committed to the Source of all good things, who holds the universe in his hand and by his providence can be relied upon to do all things well. Is this your experience?

I have left a couple of loopholes of doubt. We all *tend* to be idolatrous and, *in theory*, Christians have turned their backs on idolatry. But what is the hard-core reality?

I believe that for most Christians – and I mean genuinely born-again, committed, regenerate Christians, not merely the occasional church-goers or hesitant fellow-travellers — the idol-centred natural instincts are much more influential than we care to imagine. For some of us they exert a more powerful influence than the Spirit of God. We don't see it because we don't want to see it, but we allow our idol-fears and selfish prayers to be dressed up in Christian clothes. We add 'In Christ's name, Amen' to our self-centred petitions and see as God's activity whatever makes us feel comfortable and as satanic interference whatever we don't like.

You may wish to protest that the true Christian has renounced evil in every shape or form and that the truly regenerate person, made new by the Spirit of God, cannot be held in thrall by the power of darkness. Does it not say in Scripture, 'Those who have been born of God do not sin, because God's seed abides in them; they cannot sin, because they have been born of God' (1 John 3:9)? Yes, but did not the same author say two chapters previously, 'If we say that we have no sin, we deceive ourselves, and the truth is not in us' (1 John 1:8)? The whole body of Paul's letters, as well as John's, Peter's and James's, is directed to warning the young churches about various kinds of sin. Paul knew the strength of the opposition: 'For our struggle is not against enemies of blood and flesh, but against the rulers, against the authorities, against the cosmic powers of this present darkness, against the spiritual forces of evil in the heavenly places' (Ephesians 6:12).

It's not a straight choice of doing a right thing or doing a wrong thing, it's a question of whether we are being constantly renewed in the Spirit of God which makes us humbly to love God and desire what he wants us to do, or being dragged down by our natural instincts which are idolatrous and make us afraid of God and try to get him to do what we want. And for most of us the latter influence is very strong indeed.

This being so, perhaps it is not so strange that John finishes his first letter so apparently abruptly and off the point. It is not off the point at all and is of vital importance. 1 John 5:21 reads: 'Little children, keep yourselves from idols.'

As we have seen, the greatest sick-joke of all is that we have destroyed our idol-shelves and our demon-things; we have turned our backs on the idolatry of hero-worship, wealth, fame and fortune and have directed our idol-worship towards God himself. Our *image* of God is more real to us than the real God; and we worship it, instead of him.

Incarnation or incanration

I can't remember where I saw the misprint, a simple switch of the letters r and n, but the word 'incanration' has stayed with me ever since. Perhaps it can convey the contrast between God becoming flesh for us and our desire to have God 'in the can'.

Two hundred years ago and more, opera was very popular in Europe. Extravagant and elaborate stories, often culled from classical times, were set to music. Tenors serenaded their lovers *fortissimo* while all the neighbours slept in peace, and contraltos died impressively on stage, again singing at full volume; all totally unrealistic. Equally unreal, but very impressive, were the mechanical effects which astonished the audience; fire and brimstone, volcanic eruptions, flying fairies (and harpies), ideas borrowed from the ancient Greek theatre but ingeniously developed to the delight of the opera-going public.

A favourite device of the time was the *deus ex machina*, the god out of the machinery. The heroine, and perhaps the hero too, became hopelessly entangled in the wiles of the villain until it was clear that all was lost and then, at the very last moment, a deity in a basket would be lowered on to the stage, the happy pair would be whisked to safety out of the very clutches of their captor. Sometimes it was more subtle than this, but the phrase *deus ex machina* has come to describe any device or event that arrives in the nick of time to avert disaster.

What has all this to do with the incarnation? I think this: that we instinctively desire God to be a *deus ex machina* for us, to come into our world and miraculously rescue us from the tangles and disasters we are stuck with. Our prayer, like that of the psalmists of old, is that God would 'rend the heavens and come down', heal me from this illness, give peace of mind to the depressed, feed the hungry, abolish warfare and let us all have joy and prosperity.

All of this is what the prophets foretold will happen. It is all focused and distilled in the Song of Mary, recorded in Luke chapter 1. When told that she was to be the mother of God's Son, and after getting over the initial shock, she responded in praise to God for choosing such a humble person as herself for such an exalted task and saw the role of her Son to be in terms of the salvation of the poor and 'come-uppance' for the dictators of the world:

He has shown strength with his arm;
  he has scattered the proud in the thoughts of their hearts.
He has brought down the powerful from their thrones,
  and lifted up the lowly.
He has filled the hungry with good things,
  and sent the rich away empty . . .

(Luke 1:51–53)

So God has rent the heavens and come down, but in his own way, not in the way that we expect, or perhaps hope. He came as a helpless baby. That should have given us the hint. He was poor, persecuted and misunderstood. Certainly he healed and forgave and lifted up the downtrodden, but as the story unfolds it becomes clear that instead of descending in a divine basket to solve all our problems, the Son of God came to us to share in the problems. He is not a god out of a machine to whisk us out of this hard world, he is God in flesh, enduring and suffering the world with us and on our behalf.

This doesn't match up to what we want. We wanted an idol who would do our will: we find ourselves with a God who asks us to conform to his will. We wanted 'god-up-there' and we find we have God-down-here, disturbingly close.

This all sounds rather depressing but, when we try to see it all from God's point of view, a positive understanding emerges.

For a start, Jesus *was* persecuted, even to death. He experienced everything that the world could throw at him, so we cannot accuse him of not understanding ('. . . the suffering of death, so that by the grace of God he might taste death for everyone', Hebrews 2:9). But death could not hold him. He came back and by his Spirit becomes ever more closely 'God with us' than before. Many sufferers have said that they longed for relief but that the relief of knowing that God was with them in it was greater than would have been their feeling of desertion if they had been cured and yet lost the presence of God.

So was Mary's song a pipe-dream or just meant to be taken figuratively? Or was it looking forward to that Last Day when all our wounds are to be bound up, all tears dried and everything set to rights? That day has not yet come. The life, death and resurrection of Christ did not save the world. Yet. But our faith is that one day it will.

Meanwhile . . .

Meanwhile our task is to see that we grow in true faith and that our natural idol-seeking nature is starved of the food that it grows on: fear and greed. In the final chapter we shall be looking at some directions that may help us to become more thoroughly rid of this nature. But let it not be thought that this is an easy fix. All along the line we are in danger of confusion because the way to idolatry looks so similar to the way to God.

We have just stated that our natural deep-down desire is to have Someone to do what we can't do for ourselves and to please Someone by doing good. Is this the slippery slope to idolatry or is it the definition of the 'God-shaped blank' that will lead us to heaven? The answer is, of course, 'both'. It's the way things are and it's up to us which way we choose to react.

And if I can't analyse every moment of the day how I ought to react, can I not hope to become more and more God-centred and less and less idol-ridden?

Stories are told, especially concerning the Second World War, of spies who were wonderfully fluent in German, French or English (depending whose side they were on), but whose native language was not the one they were speaking. One of the tests to discover their native tongue was to administer a sudden and painful shock. Without the chance to think about it, their reaction would be perfectly 'natural'. These agents had to be so changed within by their training that the language they spoke became as 'natural' as their own, in fact became their new 'natural' language.

So with us. If idol-seeking is 'natural', we need the constant loving influence of the Holy Spirit to turn our instincts into alien responses and our new instincts of love and glad service will become natural to us, and we are at home in him. But it is a life-time's process.

CHAPTER 15

The most excellent way

Any serious discussion about making changes in ourselves will be useless if we are not convinced of the need for change. All that has been said so far in this book suggests that there is a need. As the reader you must make up your own mind, but it seems to me that the distinctiveness of the 'new' lifestyle which Christians profess is often only skin deep and never profound enough. We frequently mistake the means for the end and concentrate on secondary issues instead of worshipping God. And when we do approach God we try to manipulate and to placate him.

So if we are in earnest about improving the situation, we have to admit that there is a problem and (this is the hard one) also be flexible in our thinking and attitudes, willing to make some changes in ourselves (or to allow God to make them for us). We shall need to be more broad-minded and willing to understand what God is saying to us as we read the Bible, not merely what other people tell us that he is saying. What is true for them may not be precisely true for you.

Certainly our faith is based on objective facts which are equally true for all of us. God came into the world in Jesus Christ. His death and resurrection opened the gate into his kingdom. His Spirit has been poured out, so that we can rely on his real presence. We are all basically flawed and need God to rescue us from our self-centred alienation from him and from each other.

But the fact also remains that he meets each of us as unique people. His way with you is not his way with me. His approach to the woman at the well, to Zacchaeus, to Mary, to Martha, to any of the individuals he met and whom we meet in the pages of the New Testament was different in each case.

Christianity is a corporate religion. In other words, it calls us together in community (we shall say more about this presently), but the community is made up of unique individuals. The first step away from idolatry is to know more clearly what is my relationship with God; to know who I am.

Who am I?

How many of us wish we knew the answer to that question. Alice, during her adventures in Wonderland, was confused by the Caterpillar, who sat smoking on top of his mushroom, by the question 'Who are you?' She had to confess that she hardly knew. She seemed to have been several different people during the day. This is often our own experience too.

Am I defined by my job or lack of a job? By how much I do or do not earn? By my title, Right Reverend, Sir, Excellency, Mr or Mrs, Ms or just plain Jim or Kate? I am son, or daughter, to somebody. Does that explain and define who I am? Am I only 'somebody' if I have made a scratch on the surface of the world, made a million pounds/Marks/dollars, invented something, founded a movement or appeared on TV? If none of these things, then the question returns, 'Who am I?'

The answer is that I am a child of God. He created the world I inhabit. He invented the reproductive system by which I was born. He therefore gave me life. Moreover he loved me so much that he sent his Son Jesus Christ to die on my behalf (see John 3:1–21). In that I have gladly accepted his love for me, though it was totally undeserved, he has given me the right to consider myself one of the family (John 1:10–13). So I know who I am, in the deepest possible sense: a member of God's family by his gracious adoption. I may often wonder what I am doing or what part I should be playing or where I am going, but I can be secure in knowing the most important fact of all: who I am.

And by this process of understanding I am coming to know who God is too. He has asked me to call him Father (see Matthew 6:9–15). I don't know much about God but that is enough. He is my Father. This is only basic Christian teaching, but if it is thoroughly understood and freely accepted it is mind-blowing and has dramatic implications.

If I am quite clear in my own mind and also comfortable in my feelings that God is my Father and I am God's child, then I am less likely to treat God as an idol. He is real; he is alive; he is the source of my life itself as well as of my renewed spiritual life. So I belong to him. He does not belong to me. I cannot presume to direct him in what is best for the world, or even for myself. He knows what is best and I have to look to him to bring it about.

And since this relationship with all its wonderful implications is entirely his doing and by his undeserved grace, it would be a gross impertinence for me to try to influence him by bringing little bribes, trying to please him in order to 'deserve' some benefit. It would be like a small child bringing teacher a sticky sweet in exchange for some favour in school. In an adult it would be a pathetic attempt at idolatry.

We are well on the road to recovery from idolizing God if we know who we are and who he is. But it is important to know, not just to understand. I mentioned above the need to be comfortable in my feelings. Please don't dismiss this as psycho-clap-trap. It is very easy for Christians to say a creed, agree to a list of beliefs, without actually 'internalizing' them, without their being taken fully on board, without their taking possession of the mainspring of our will. In this case they do not change our attitudes. They are mere wallpaper when the whole house needed rebuilding.

In his play *No Exit*, Jean-Paul Sartre gives us a vision of hell. Three people discover the guilty truth about one another. But there is nothing more – for ever, just guilty truth. You are your life, and nothing else. But in Christ we are not just our life. There is much more. We are ourselves *plus* what God has made us for and will cause us to be.

This basic knowledge that I am a child of God, fully understood, felt, internalized and acted upon is very profound. There are many people who cannot take it on board because of deep hurts in the past which block off their acceptance of son/daughtership. If you are in this category please be humble and honest enough to get wise help from a pastor or counsellor. For others, the understanding may come in a flash. Yet others will need to pray and think and wrestle with the idea until it becomes clearer. But it is all eminently worthwhile and will set our relationship with God on a firm footing.

Who is God?

The second major step away from idolizing God which I want to suggest may be unexpected and is certainly paradoxical. Once we have fully grasped who we are, that we have meaning and personhood purely because we have a relationship with God, we need to explore the nature of God a little more. What is he like? Will he treat us like the patriarchal father-figure in all the old stories, forbidding us to talk at meal-times, ordering us to serve him in the most unpleasant ways, always demanding our obedience and subservience?

At a first glance this would appear to be a likely answer. If an idol is something we try to manipulate, to get it to do what we want, then surely the opposite is a God who manipulates us, who gets us to do what he wants. There is a degree of truth here of course. God called us to pray 'Our Father . . . your will be done.' But his will is to be done because it is best for him and for us, not because he wants to 'pull rank' on us, to use his almightiness to beat us about the head with.

So what is God like? Christlike. John V. Taylor, quoting the late Archbishop Ramsey, has entitled a book '*The Christlike God*'. 'Whoever has seen me has seen the Father,' said Jesus (John 14:9). He came to show us what God is like. One of the most striking of all his demonstrations is recorded in John chapter 13. John prefaces his narrative by noting that what Jesus did was to begin to show his disciples the full extent of his love. The completion of that demonstration was to be on the cross of Calvary.

The Last Supper had been arranged and for some reason there was no servant available to perform the usual foot-washing for the guests. The disciples sat tight – no-one was willing to make a move. Then Jesus himself took a towel and performed the menial act for them, shaming them all no doubt, but more importantly showing us that this God whom we worship comes among us to serve us. To serve us. This bears repeating because it is quite staggering to imagine the Lord of the Universe offering to wash my dirty feet. It doesn't make sense. How often have we sung Graham Kendrick's justly loved hymn 'This is our God, the Servant King' without realizing fully what it is, or rather Who it is, we are singing about?

If Jesus came to reveal to us what God is like then God wants to serve us.

Yes, there will come a time when every knee shall bow and every tongue confess that Jesus Christ is Lord, and yes, every Christian wants to do God's will because he is God and we know it to be the best way for us, but he still comes to us as the Servant King. The God who thundered on Mount Sinai to the terror of Israel was the same God who spoke to Isaiah the astonishing words, 'Come, let us reason together', sit down with me and consider what I am saying. Jesus told parables and asked, 'What do you think then?' If he was God why did he not say, 'Do this, or else'? God is Christlike.

If we can fully grasp how loving and really *thoughtful* and gracious it is of God to approach us in this way, surely we cannot treat him as an idol, taking advantage of him and trying to 'twist his arm' to get what we want. It is almost unthinkable.

No, we are moved to thanksgiving rather, and praise and worship in sheer gratitude for God's coming down from his heavenly throne and living with us. We saw earlier that praise and worship which flows from gratitude is a good antidote to idolatry. Consider the difference between our response to a glittering-eyed statue which might give me what I want if I do enough to please it and Jesus Christ who approaches us with a smile of welcome and a towel over his arm.

I wrote 'approaches *us*' intentionally because there is another paradox here. Although each of us is unique (he comes to us individually and we respond individually), yet we are gathered into the community of believers and become part of his body. When we are reconciled to him we are reconciled to each other and can worship him together, in true fellowship and *shalom* (see page 54). Idol-worship is often individualistic; true worship is corporate.

A final point. Jesus comes to serve us. Yes, but he is not at our beck and call. He serves us on his own terms. When Peter reacted to Jesus' offer to wash his feet by saying, 'Not just my feet but my head and my hands as well', wanting something on his terms, Jesus said, No. True prayer tries to discern what God wants us to have and then asks for it. Idol-prayer asks for what I want and tries to persuade God to let me have it.

And finally

The third and decisive step away from idolizing God is the step of love; what Paul described in 1 Corinthians 12:31 as 'the most excellent way'. It is well known that the kind of love that Paul described in the following chapter is a self-giving, active, generous love, not a slushy feeling or an erotic passion, nor even the passive love of someone for scenery or basketwork. Real love is open, up-building and fulfilling. It is what we are put on the earth for, to express the character of God: for God *is* love.

We have noticed before that a major characteristic of idolatry is fear. We try to buy the spirit because we fear the consequences. 'There is no fear in love,' wrote John in his first letter (4:18), 'but perfect love casts out fear; for fear has to do with punishment.'

Writer Joyce Huggett quotes a letter from a Chinese young man which sums it up to perfection. He says, 'I had been brought up to believe in many gods – all hostile. They needed to be placated with food and money, otherwise they would be angry. But now I know that God loves me. It's marvellous.'

In this world we shall probably never be fully free from the tendency to demand what we want and to try to placate God, perhaps more subtly than with food or money. But if we know who we are in our relationship to him, what he is like in his relations with us and something of the love that binds us together in fellowship with each other and with him, then idolatry will be well and truly on the run.

And even if we do fall back into demanding things purely for ourselves (and we certainly shall!) it is a great comfort to know that 'he who is faithful and just will forgive us our sins' (1 John 1:9). Moreover we can be confident that in his mercy he will refuse to answer these ill-advised prayers. How grateful I am for the fatherly twinkle in the eye of God when he hears my panic-stricken, self-centred demands and says, in effect, 'One day you'll see the folly of that prayer – for the moment I shall look the other way.'

Let us pray that our wrong-headed prayers will never be answered. As the anonymous writer put it:

I asked God for strength that I might achieve,
   but I was made weak that I might learn humility.
I asked for health that I might do great things,
   but was given infirmity that I might do better things.
I asked for riches that I might be happy,
   but I was given poverty that I might be wise.
I asked for things that I might enjoy life,
   but I was given life that I might enjoy things.
I got nothing that I asked for, but everything that I hoped for.
   Despite myself, my prayers were answered.
I am amongst all people most richly blessed.

A personal postscript

How does all this work out in practice? It's not for me to presume to tell you how to relate to God or to other people; I can only tell you how it has worked for me and hope that it will help you. If it doesn't, all is not lost.

It is usually easier for people to recognize that they are part of God's family if they have enjoyed a good childhood experience in their own family. I think I was fortunate there, but it only began to dawn on me that I was (or needed to be) acceptable to God when I joined a Crusader Bible class as a teenager and found that the people there were concerned for me, not just as a statistic but as a person. That part of the family of God, of the body of Christ, was expressing to me what God was saying. 'My child, I have adopted you. Come in and be welcome.' The realization came very slowly, but it has never left me. It helps me to know who I am.

Then, for me, who is God? God was holy (he still is) and difficult to approach, so one always needed to confess one's sins before daring to pray. There's a lot of truth in this of course – beware of getting too chummy with the Almighty. One evening as I headed home from work on the Metropolitan-line train, somewhere near Finchley Road I think it was, I realized that I had neither book nor newspaper to read. Bother! I suppose I'd better pray instead. With a sigh I sat up straighter, put my hands in my lap, lowered my eyelids (a little) and prepared to think of something to be repentant about, when a voice, very nearly audible, said clearly to my mind, 'We've had a good day together today, Derek.' I have never thought of God as less than holy since then but I also know that he is approachable and much closer at hand than I had thought, and he's interested in *me*.

Now what about loving God? Can I claim to love God? I confess that I find it hard to join in the singing of 'How I love you, Lord'. How can I know that I love God when I cannot see him? I can respect him, worship him, fear him even and I know that he loves me. I think John, in his first letter, understood my predicament. Perhaps he had the same problem himself. In chapter 4, verses 10 to 12, he writes:

> In this is love, not that we loved God but that he loved us and sent his Son to be the atoning sacrifice for our sins. Beloved, since God loved us so much, we also ought to love one another. No one has ever seen God; if we love one another, God lives in us, and his love is perfected in us.

and in verses 19–21:

> We love because he first loved us. Those who say, 'I love God,' and hate their brothers and sisters, are liars; for those who do not love a brother or sister whom they have seen, cannot love God whom they have not seen. The commandment we have from him is this: those who love God must love their brothers and sisters also.

John is not saying that you can love God *only* by loving other people but he is clear that if you don't love other people you cannot claim to be loving God. Love for

God and for members of his family are very closely tied together and it is hard to disentangle them. I think that I am gradually learning to love people more, so perhaps I am loving God too. I hope so.

If my experience doesn't help you, so be it, but let us pray that we shall all come to shun the 'god' which is useful to us, or which rules us through fear, and come to worship and to love the Christ-like God who comes alongside us by his Spirit and in his love walks with us along the way to eternity. We dare not try to persuade him to do our bidding but then, if he really is God, it's much better for all concerned if we can't.